YOUR PERSONAL
HOROSCOPE
2017

♏

SCORPIO

YOUR PERSONAL
HOROSCOPE
2017

SCORPIO

24th October–22nd November

igloobooks

igloobooks

Published in 2016
by Igloo Books Ltd
Cottage Farm
Sywell
NN6 0BJ
www.igloobooks.com

Produced for Igloo Books by Foulsham Publishing Ltd, The Old Barrel Store,
Drayman's Lane, Marlow, Bucks SL7 2FF, England

FIR003 0716
2 4 6 8 10 9 7 5 3 1
ISBN: 978-1-78557-896-0

This is an abridged version of material originally published
in Old Moore's Horoscope and Astral Diary.

Cover images: iStock
Cover designed by Nicholas Gage

Printed and manufactured in China

CONTENTS

INTRODUCTION

Your Personal Horoscopes have been specifically created to allow you to get the most from astrological patterns and the way they have a bearing on not only your zodiac sign, but nuances within it. Using the diary section of the book you can read about the influences and possibilities of each and every day of the year. It will be possible for you to see when you are likely to be cheerful and happy or those times when your nature is in retreat and you will be more circumspect. The diary will help to give you a feel for the specific 'cycles' of astrology and the way they can subtly change your day-to-day life. For example, when you see the sign ☿, this means that the planet Mercury is retrograde at that time. Retrograde means it appears to be running backwards through the zodiac. Such a happening has a significant effect on communication skills, but this is only one small aspect of how the Personal Horoscope can help you.

With Your Personal Horoscope the story doesn't end with the diary pages. It includes simple ways for you to work out the zodiac sign the Moon occupied at the time of your birth, and what this means for your personality. In addition, if you know the time of day you were born, it is possible to discover your Ascendant, yet another important guide to your personal make-up and potential.

Many readers are interested in relationships and in knowing how well they get on with people of other astrological signs. You might also be interested in the way you appear to very different sorts of individuals. If you are such a person, the section on Venus will be of particular interest. Despite the rapidly changing position of this planet, you can work out your Venus sign, and learn what bearing it will have on your life.

Using Your Personal Horoscope you can travel on one of the most fascinating and rewarding journeys that anyone can take – the journey to a better realisation of self.

THE ESSENCE OF SCORPIO

Exploring the Personality of Scorpio the Scorpion

(24TH OCTOBER–22ND NOVEMBER)

What's in a sign?

To say that you are a little complicated and somewhat difficult to understand is probably a great understatement. The basic reason for this lies in the peculiar nature of Scorpio rulership. In terms of the elements, your zodiac sign is a Water sign. This makes you naturally emotional, deep, somewhat reserved and ever anxious to help those around you. As a direct contrast, classical astrologers always maintained that your planetary ruler was Mars. Mars is the planet of combat and aggression, being positive and dominant under most circumstances. So it can be judged from the start that there are great contradictions within the basic Scorpio nature.

It's a fact that many people are naturally cautious of Scorpio people. Perhaps this isn't surprising. Under most circumstances you appear to be quiet and peaceful, but the situation is a little like a smoking bomb. When it comes to defending yourself, or in particular those people who you see as being important to you, there is virtually no limit to which you would refuse to go. Generally speaking our ancient ancestors were extremely wise in terms of the names they gave to the different zodiac signs. Consider the apparently diminutive and retiring scorpion. It doesn't go looking for trouble and is generally happy to remain in the shadows. However, if it is provoked, or even attacked, it will take on adversaries many times its own size. It carries a barbed sting in its tail and will strike without any additional warning if necessary.

All the same, the Scorpio reputation may be a little undeserved. Yours is one of the most compassionate and caring of all the zodiac signs. When it comes to working on behalf of humanity, especially the oppressed, the sick or the disenfranchised, you show your true mettle. You cannot stand the thought of people suffering unjustifiably, which is why many of the great social reformers and even freedom fighters had the same zodiac sign as you do.

As a Scorpio you are likely to be intuitive (some would say psychic) and under most circumstances you are more than willing to follow that little voice inside yourself that tells you how to behave in any given situation.

Scorpio resources

Your nature is so very often understated that it might be said that your greatest resource is surprise. You have the ability to shock people constantly, even those who think they understand you perfectly well. This brings us back to the creature for which your zodiac sign is named. A scorpion is diminutive – and would represent a tasty snack for any would-be predator. However, it defies logic by standing its ground and fighting back. When it does, woe betide the aggressor that refuses to take account of its presence. And so it is with you. Quiet, even reserved, you tend to get on with your work. This you do efficiently and without undue fuss, approaching each task with the same methodical attitude. People often don't even realise that you are around. And then, when they least expect it, there you are!

The ability to surprise means that you often get on in life against heavy odds. In addition you have great resilience and fortitude. It is possible for you to continue to work long and hard under circumstances that would force others to retreat. Most Scorpio people would not consider themselves to be tough – in fact quite a few are positively neurotic when it comes to matters associated with their own health. Yet you can endure hardship well and almost always win through in the end.

It's true that you may not be quite as confident as you could be. If you were, people would notice you more and that would detract from that all-important element of surprise that makes you so formidable, and which is definitely the most important weapon in your armoury. However, it is clear that your greatest resource is compassion, and on those occasions when you really allow it to show, you display yourself as being one of the most important allies to your fellow men and women.

At a practical level you are more than capable and can often be expected to perform tasks that you haven't necessarily undertaken before. You have a deep intelligence and good powers to reason things out. Most important of all is a determination that no other zodiac sign can match.

Beneath the surface

This section of an account of the typical Scorpio nature could fill an entire book in itself because you are such a complicated person. However, there are certain advantages to being a Scorpio. For example, nobody is going to run away with the idea that you are basically uncomplicated and shallow. It ought to be clear enough to the dullest observer that there is a boiling, seething volcano bubbling away beneath the surface of almost every Scorpio subject.

You are often accused of having a slightly dark view of life, and it's true that many Scorpio people enjoy a rather morbid curiosity and are fascinated by subjects that make other people shudder. At the same time you could hardly be described as being one of life's natural optimists. Part of the reason for this lies in the fact that you have been disappointed in the past and may have arrived at the conclusion that to expect the worst is often the most sensible course of action. At least that way you are likely to mitigate some of the potential depression regarding failures in the future.

Although this way of thinking is somewhat faulty, it comes so naturally to the Scorpio subject that it actually works very well, though it has to be said that it might be responsible for a tendency to hold back on occasions.

Assessing the way your inner mind works is as difficult for you as it is for any outsider. Even individuals who have been friends for years will sometimes come desperately unstuck if they arrive at the conclusion that they know well what makes you tick. In the recesses of your mind you are passionate, driving, restless, dissatisfied and frequently disappointed with your own efforts. On the other hand, you have the power to make dreams into realities and are excellent at hatching plans that will benefit people far from your own circle and circumstances. Being a tireless worker on behalf of the oppressed, the fate of humanity as a whole is ever an inner concern.

When you love you do so with great width and depth. Your capacity for jealousy knows no bounds and there are times when you can be as destructive to yourself as you ever could be regarding any other individual. Yet for all this your inner mind is lofty and can soar like an eagle on occasions. If the world at large was able to fathom just one tenth of the way your inner mind actually works, people would find you even more fascinating than they do already. But perhaps it's best that they don't. The deepest recesses of Scorpio are an intense secret and will usually stay that way.

Making the best of yourself

It isn't hard to find a single word that describes the way you can make the best of yourself, especially when viewed by the world at large. That word is 'communication'. When difficulties arise in your life, especially concerning other people, it's usually because you haven't managed to get your message across, and probably because you haven't even tried to do so. There is much to your nature that is electric, powerful and magnetic. These qualities make you potentially popular and fascinating to a wealth of individuals. Hide these qualities beneath too brusque an exterior and you can seem dark and brooding.

Of course it's a fine line and one that isn't easy to walk. You are constantly worried that if you show people what really makes you tick, they will not find you interesting at all. In reality this concern is totally without foundation. There is more than enough depth about you to last several lifetimes. It doesn't matter how much you give of yourself to the world at large, there are always going to be surprises galore to follow.

Use the dynamic qualities of your nature to the full. Traditionally your ruling planet is Mars – a real go-getter of a planetary ruler and one that imbues you with tremendous power to get things done at a practical level. On the way you need to show how much you care about others. Amidst a plethora of gifts offered to you by the celestial spheres, your ability to help others is likely to be top of the list. When you are giving you are also usually approachable. For you the two go hand in hand. Avoid allowing yourself to become morose or inward looking and always strive to find simple answers to simple questions.

Stick to some sort of work that you find interesting. That can be almost anything to a Scorpio, as long as it feeds the inner you. It does need to carry a degree of diversity and should ideally have an end product that is easy to see. On your journey through life don't get carried away with daydreams – yet on the other hand avoid losing your great potential to make them come true.

The impressions you give

This is one area of your life over which you do have a great deal of control. If the adage 'what you see is what you get' turns out to be true for many signs of the zodiac, it certainly isn't the case with you. The complexity of your nature makes it difficult for even you to find 'the real Scorpio', and in any case this tends to change from day to day. However, regarding some matters there isn't any doubt at all. Firstly you are deeply magnetic and possess the ability to arouse an instinctive fascination in others. Ally this to your propensity for being very positive in your decision making and you have a potentially formidable combination.

Most people already think of you as being an extremely interesting person. Unfortunately they may also occasionally consider you to be a little cool and somewhat difficult to approach. Neither of these impressions are true, it's simply that you are quite shy at heart, and sometimes find it difficult to believe that you could be liked by certain individuals. Learn to throw this erroneous assumption out of the window, and instead, expect to be viewed positively. To do so would make all the difference and would clear the way so that your more personable side can show all the time.

Very few people who know you well could fail to realise that you care deeply, especially about the well-being of the oppressed. You have a truly noble spirit, a fact that shines through in practically everything you do – yet another reason to be noticed.

It's true that you can sometimes make your secretive quality into an art form, which those looking in from the outside might find rather difficult to deal with. This represents another outward aspect of your nature that could so easily be altered. By all means keep your secrets, though not about matters that are of no real note whatsoever. In a single phrase, try to lighten up a little. It's all you need to be almost perfect!

The way forward

It must first be held in mind that Scorpio people are complicated. That's something you simply cannot get away from, no matter how much you might try. On the one hand you can deal with practical matters almost instinctively. You are resourceful, deep thinking, intense and fascinating. On the other side of the coin you are often too fond of luxury and will frequently withdraw yourself from situations that you do not care to pursue. You can be quite stubborn and can even bear a grudge if you feel that you have been provoked.

It is suggested in astrology that no quality of nature is necessarily good or bad, it really depends on the way it is used. For example, stubbornness can be considered a terrible fault, but not if you were being awkward concerning the obvious rights of an oppressed person or group. It turns out that Scorpio has more of a potential to be 'saint or sinner' than any zodiac sign. As long as you examine your motives in any given situation, whilst at the same time trying to cultivate a degree of flexibility that is not one of your natural gifts, then you won't go far wrong.

Turn on the charm when it is necessary because it will rarely if ever let you down. Think about the way you can serve the world, but don't preach about it. Love sincerely, but don't allow jealousy to spoil things. Be constructive in your determination and don't get on your high horse when it isn't necessary. Follow these simple rules for the best chance of progress.

Of course there are many positives around to start with. You are a very loyal friend, are capable of being extremely brave and tend to be very committed to family members. At the same time you are trustworthy and can work long and hard using your own initiative. Although you sometimes worry about your health, you are more robust than most and can endure a high degree of hardship if necessary. You don't take kindly to criticism but can be flexible enough to accept it if you know it is intended for your own good.

Few people doubt your sincerity – that is, when they know what you believe. So it's important to lay your thoughts on the line right from the start. And even if you don't choose to treat the whole world as a friend, you are capable of gathering a little circle around you who would never let you down. Do make sure, however, that this 'inner group' isn't simply comprised of other Scorpios!

SCORPIO ON THE CUSP

Astrological profiles are altered for those people born at either the beginning or the end of a zodiac sign, or, more properly, on the cusps of a sign. In the case of Scorpio this would be on the 24th of October and for two or three days after, and similarly at the end of the sign, probably from the 20th to the 22nd of November.

The Libra Cusp – 24th to 26th October

You are probably generally considered to be a bright and breezy sort of character, with a great deal of enthusiasm for life. Despite this, few people would doubt that you are a shrewd operator, and that you know what you want and have a fairly good idea of how to go about getting it. Not everyone likes you as much as you would wish, but that's because the Libran side of your nature longs for popularity, while set against this is your deep Scorpio need to speak your mind, even when you know that other people might wish you did not indulge in this trait very frequently.

In love, you typify the split between these two signs. On the one hand you are passionate, sincere and intense, while on the other your Libran responses can cause a certain fickle sort of affection to show sometimes, probably to the confusion of those with whom you are involved at a personal level. Nevertheless, few people would find fault with your basic nature and there isn't much doubt that your heart is in the right place.

When it comes to career matters, you have a very fortunate combination. Scorpio can sometimes be accused of lacking diplomacy, but nothing could be further from the truth with Libra. As a result, you have what it takes in terms of determination but at the same time you are capable of seeing the point of view put forward by colleagues. You tend to rise to the top of the tree and, with your mixture of raw ability and humour that most of the world approves of, you can stay there.

You won't be the sort of person to make quite as many enemies as Scorpio taken alone might do, and you need the cut and thrust of the world much more than the retiring creature after whom your zodiac sign is named. Try not to be controversial and do your best to retain a sense of humour, which is essential to your well-being. Few would doubt the fact that your heart is in the right place and your creative potential could be second to none. Most important of all, you need the self-satisfaction that comes from living in the real world.

The Sagittarius Cusp – 20th to 22nd November

You can be a really zany character, with a love of life that is second to none. Add to this a penetrating insight, a razor-sharp wit and an instinctive intuition that is quite remarkable and we find in you a formidable person. It's true that not everyone understands what makes you tick, probably least of all yourself, but you strive to be liked and really do want to advertise your willingness to learn and to grow, which isn't always the province of Scorpio when taken alone. Your capacity for work knows no bounds, though you don't really like to get your hands dirty and would feel more content when telling others what to do.

In a career sense, you need to be in a position from which you are able to delegate. This is not because you are afraid of hard work yourself, far from it, but you possess a strong ability to see through problems and you are a natural director of others. Sales careers may interest you, or a position from which you can organise and arrange things. However, you hate to be tied down to one place for long, so you would be at your best when allowed to move around freely and do things in your own way.

You are a natural social reformer, mainly because you are sure that you know what is right and just. In the main you are correct in your assumptions, but there are occasions when you should realise that there is more than one form of truth. Perhaps you are not always quite as patient with certain individuals as you might be but these generally tend to be people who show traits of cruelty or cunning. As a family person, you care very much for the people who figure most prominently in your life. Sometimes you are a definite home bird, with a preference for what you know and love, but this is offset by a restless trend within your nature that often sends you off into the wide blue yonder, chasing rainbows that the Scorpio side of your nature doubts are even there. Few would doubt your charm, your magnetism, or your desire to get ahead in life in almost any way possible. You combine patience with genuine talent and make a loyal, interesting and entertaining friend or lover.

SCORPIO AND ITS ASCENDANTS

The nature of every individual on the planet is composed of the rich variety of zodiac signs and planetary positions that were present at the time of their birth. Your Sun sign, which in your case is Scorpio, is one of the many factors when it comes to assessing the unique person you are. Probably the most important consideration, other than your Sun sign, is to establish the zodiac sign that was rising over the eastern horizon at the time that you were born. This is your Ascending or Rising sign. Most popular astrology fails to take account of the Ascendant, and yet its importance remains with you from the very moment of your birth, through every day of your life. The Ascendant is evident in the way you approach the world, and so, when meeting a person for the first time, it is this astrological influence that you are most likely to notice first. Our Ascending sign essentially represents what we appear to be, while the Sun sign is what we feel inside ourselves.

The Ascendant also has the potential for modifying our overall nature. For example, if you were born at a time of day when Scorpio was passing over the eastern horizon (this would be around the time of dawn) then you would be classed as a double Scorpio. As such, you would typify this zodiac sign, both internally and in your dealings with others. However, if your Ascendant sign turned out to be a Fire sign, such as Aries, there would be a profound alteration of nature, away from the expected qualities of Scorpio.

One of the reasons why popular astrology often ignores the Ascendant is that it has always been rather difficult to establish. We have found a way to make this possible by devising an easy-to-use table, which you will find on page 157 of this book. Using this, you can establish your Ascendant sign at a glance. You will need to know your rough time of birth, then it is simply a case of following the instructions.

For those readers who have no idea of their time of birth it might be worth allowing a good friend, or perhaps your partner, to read through the section that follows this introduction. Someone who deals with you on a regular basis may easily discover your Ascending sign, even though you could have some difficulty establishing it for yourself. A good understanding of this component of your nature is essential if you want to be aware of that 'other person' who is responsible for the way you make contact with the world at large. Your Sun sign, Ascendant sign, and the other pointers in this book will, together, allow you a far better understanding of what makes you tick as an individual. Peeling back the different layers of your astrological make-up can be an enlightening experience, and the Ascendant may represent one of the most important layers of all.

Scorpio with Scorpio Ascendant

This is one of the most potent of all astrological possibilities, but how it is used depends so very much on the individual who possesses it. On the one hand you are magnetic, alluring, sexy, deep and very attractive, whilst at the same time you are capable of being stubborn, self-seeking, vain, over-sensitive and fathomless. It has to be said that under most circumstances the first set of adjectives are the most appropriate, and that is because you keep control of the deeper side, refusing to allow it absolute control over your conscious life. You are able to get almost anything you want from life, but first you have to discover what that might be. The most important factor of all, however, is the way you can offer yourself, totally and without reservation to a needy world.

Self-sacrifice is a marvellous thing, but you can go too far on occasions. The furthest extreme for Scorpios here is a life that is totally dedicated to work and prayer. For the few this is admirable, for the still earth-based, less so. Finding a compromise is not easy as you are not always in touch with yourself. Feed the spiritual, curb the excesses, accept the need for luxury, and be happy.

Scorpio with Sagittarius Ascendant

There are many gains with this combination, and most of you reading this will already be familiar with the majority of them. Sagittarius offers a bright and hopeful approach to life, but may not always have the staying power and the patience to get what it really needs. Scorpio, on the other hand, can be too deep for its own good, is very self-seeking on occasions and extremely giving to others. Both the signs have problems when taken on their own, and, it has to be said, double the difficulties when they come together. But this is not usually the case. Invariably the presence of Scorpio slows down the over-quick responses of the Archer, whilst the inclusion of Sagittarius prevents Scorpio from taking itself too seriously.

Life is so often a game of extremes, when all the great spiritual masters of humanity have indicated that a 'middle way' is the path to choose. You have just the right combination of skills and mental faculties to find that elusive path, and can bring great joy to yourself and others as a result. Most of the time you are happy, optimistic, helpful and a joy to know. You have mental agility, backed up by a stunning intuition, which itself would rarely let you down. Keep a sense of proportion and understand that your depth of intellect is necessary to curb your flighty side.

Scorpio with Capricorn Ascendant

If patience, perseverance and a solid ability to get where you want to go are considered to be the chief components of a happy life, then you should be skipping about every day. Unfortunately this is not always the case and here we have two zodiac signs, both of which can be too deep for their own good. Both Scorpio and Capricorn are inclined to take themselves rather too seriously and your main lesson in life, and some would say the reason you have adopted this zodiac combination, is to 'lighten up'. If all that determination is pushed in the direction of your service to the world at large, you are seen as being one of the kindest people imaginable. This is really the only option for you, because if you turn this tremendous potential power inwards all the time you will become brooding, secretive and sometimes even selfish. Your eyes should be turned towards a needy humanity, which can be served with the dry but definite wit of Capricorn and the true compassion of Scorpio.

It is impossible with this combination to indicate what areas of life suit you the best. Certainly you adore luxury in all its forms, and yet you can get by with almost nothing. You desire travel, and at the same time love the comforts and stability of home. The people who know you best are aware that you are rather special. Listen to what they say.

Scorpio with Aquarius Ascendant

Here we have a combination that shows much promise and a flexibility that allows many changes in direction, allied to a power to succeed, sometimes very much against all the odds. Aquarius lightens the load of the Scorpio mind, turning the depths into potential and making intuitive foresight into a means for getting on in life. There are depths here, because even airy Aquarius isn't too easy to understand, and it is therefore a fact that some people with this combination will always be something of a mystery. However, even this fact can be turned to your advantage because it means that people will always be looking at you. Confidence is so often the key to success in life and the Scorpio–Aquarius mix offers this, or at least appears to do so. Even when this is not entirely the case, the fact that everyone around you believes it to be true is often enough.

You are usually good to know, and show a keen intellect and a deep intelligence, aided by a fascination for life that knows no bounds. When at your best you are giving, understanding, balanced and active. On those occasions when things are not going well for you, beware a stubborn streak and the need to be sensational. Keep it light and happy and you won't go far wrong. Most of you are very, very well loved.

Scorpio with Pisces Ascendant

You stand a chance of disappearing so deep into yourself that other people would need one of those long ladders that cave explorers use, just to find you. It isn't really your fault because both Scorpio and Pisces are Water signs, which are difficult to understand, and you have them both. But that doesn't mean that you should be content to remain in the dark, and the warmth of your nature is all you need to shine a light on the wonderful qualities you possess. But the primary word of warning is that you must put yourself on display and allow others to know what you are, before their appreciation of these facts becomes apparent.

As a server of the world you are second to none and it is hard to find a person with this combination who is not, in some way, looking out for the people around them. Immensely attractive to others, you are also one of the most sought-after lovers. Much of this has to do with your deep and abiding charm, but the air of mystery that surrounds you also helps. Some of you will marry too early, and end up regretting the fact, though the majority of people with Scorpio and Pisces will find the love they deserve in the end. You are able, just, firm but fair, though a sucker for a hard luck story and as kind as the day is long. It's hard to imagine how so many good points could be ignored by others.

Scorpio with Aries Ascendant

The two very different faces of Mars come together in this potent, magnetic and quite awe-inspiring combination. Your natural inclination is towards secrecy, and this fact, together with the natural attractions of the sensual Scorpio nature, makes you the object of great curiosity. This means that you will not go short of attention and should ensure that you are always being analysed by people who may never get to know you at all. At heart you prefer your own company, and yet life appears to find means to push you into the public gaze time and again. Most people with this combination ooze sex appeal and can use this fact as a stepping stone to personal success, yet without losing any integrity or loosening the cords of a deeply moralistic nature.

On those occasions when you do lose your temper, there isn't a character in the length and breadth of the zodiac who would have either the words or the courage to stand against the stream of invective that follows. On really rare occasions you might even scare yourself. A simple look is enough to show family members when you are not amused. Few people are left unmoved by your presence in their life.

Scorpio with Taurus Ascendant

The first, last and most important piece of advice for you is not to take yourself, or anyone else, too seriously. This might be rather a tall order because Scorpio intensifies the deeper qualities of Taurus and can make you rather lacking in the sense of humour that we all need to live our lives in this most imperfect of worlds. You are naturally sensual by nature. This shows itself in a host of ways. In all probability you can spend hours in the bath, love to treat yourself to good food and drink and take your greatest pleasure in neat and orderly surroundings. This can often alienate you from those who live in the same house because other people need to use the bathroom from time to time and they cannot remain tidy indefinitely.

You tend to worry a great deal about things which are really not too important, but don't take this statement too seriously or you will begin to worry about this fact too! You often need to lighten up and should always do your best to tell yourself that most things are not half so important as they seem to be. Be careful over the selection of a life partner and if possible choose someone who is naturally funny and who does not take life anywhere near as seriously as you are inclined to do. At work you are more than capable and in all probability everyone relies heavily on your wise judgements.

Scorpio with Gemini Ascendant

What you are and what you appear to be can be two entirely different things with this combination. Although you appear to be every bit as chatty and even as flighty as Gemini tends to be, nothing could be further from the truth. In reality you have many deep and penetrating insights, all of which are geared towards sorting out potential problems before they come along. Few people would have the ability to pull the wool over your eyes, and you show a much more astute face to the world than is often the case for Gemini taken on its own. The level of your confidence, although not earth-shattering, is much greater with this combination, and you would not be thwarted once you had made up your mind.

There is a slight danger here, however, because Gemini is always inclined to nerve problems of one sort or another. In the main these are slight and fleeting, though the presence of Scorpio can intensify reactions and heighten the possibility of depression, which would not be at all fortunate. The best way round this potential problem is to have a wealth of friends, plenty to do and the sort of variety in your life that suits your Mercury ruler. Financial success is not too difficult to achieve because you can easily earn money and then manage to hold on to it.

Scorpio with Cancer Ascendant

There are few more endearing zodiac combinations than this one. Both signs are Watery in nature and show a desire to work on behalf of humanity as a whole. The world sees you as being genuinely caring, full of sympathy for anyone in trouble and always ready to lend a hand when it is needed. You are a loyal friend, a great supporter of the oppressed and a lover of home and family. In a work sense you are capable, and command respect from your colleagues, even though this comes about courtesy of your quiet competence and not as a result of anything that you might happen to say.

But we should not get too carried away with external factors, or the way that others see you. Inside you are a boiling pool of emotion. You feel more strongly, love more deeply and hurt more fully than any other combination of the Water signs. Even those who think they know you really well would get a shock if they could take a stroll around the deeper recesses of your mind. Although these facts are true, they may be rather beside the point because it is a fact that the truth of your passion, commitment and deep convictions may only surface fully half a dozen times in your life. The fact is that you are a very private person at heart and you don't know how to be any other way.

Scorpio with Leo Ascendant

A Leo with intensity, that's what you are. You are mad about good causes and would argue the hind leg off a donkey in defence of your many ideals. If you are not out there saving the planet you could just be at home in the bath, thinking up the next way to save humanity from its own worst excesses. In your own life, although you love little luxuries, you are sparing and frugal, yet generous as can be to those you take to. It's a fact that you don't like everyone, and of course the same is true in reverse. It might be easier for you to understand why you can dislike than to appreciate the reverse side of the coin, for your pride can be badly dented on occasions. Scorpio brings a tendency to have down spells, though the fact that Leo is also strongly represented in your nature should prevent them from becoming a regular part of your life.

It is important for you to learn how to forgive and forget, and there isn't much point in bearing a grudge because you are basically too noble to do so. If something goes wrong, kiss the situation goodbye and get on with the next interesting adventure, of which there are many in your life. Stop–start situations sometimes get in the way, but there are plenty of people around who would be only too willing to lend a helping hand.

Scorpio with Virgo Ascendant

This is intensity carried through to the absolute. If you have a problem, it is that you fail to externalise all that is going on inside that deep, bubbling cauldron that is your inner self. Realising what you are capable of is not a problem; these only start when you have to make it plain to those around you what you want. Part of the reason for this is that you don't always understand yourself. You love intensely and would do absolutely anything for a person you are fond of, even though you might have to inconvenience yourself a great deal on the way. Relationships can cause you slight problems however, since you need to associate with people who at least come somewhere near to understanding what makes you tick. If you manage to bridge the gap between yourself and the world that constantly knocks on your door, you show yourself to be powerful, magnetic and compulsive.

There are times when you definitely prefer to stay quiet, though you do have a powerful ability to get your message across when you think it is necessary to do so. There are people around who might think that you are a push-over but they could easily get a shock when you sense that the time is right to answer back. You probably have a very orderly house and don't care for clutter of any sort.

Scorpio with Libra Ascendant

There is some tendency for you to be far more deep than the average Libran would appear to be and for this reason it is crucial that you lighten up from time to time. Every person with a Scorpio quality needs to remember that there is a happy and carefree side to all events and your Libran quality should allow you to bear this in mind. Sometimes you try to do too many things at the same time. This is fine if you take the casual overview of Libra, but less sensible when you insist on picking the last bone out of every potential, as is much more the case for Scorpio.

When worries come along, as they sometimes will, be able to listen to what your friends have to say and also realise that they are more than willing to work on your behalf, if only because you are so loyal to them. You do have a quality of self-deception, but this should not get in the way too much if you combine the instinctive actions of Libra with the deep intuition of your Scorpio component.

Probably the most important factor of this combination is your ability to succeed in a financial sense. You make a good manager, but not of the authoritarian sort. Jobs in the media or where you are expected to make up your mind quickly would suit you, because there is always an underpinning of practical sense that rarely lets you down.

THE MOON AND THE PART IT PLAYS IN YOUR LIFE

In astrology the Moon is probably the single most important heavenly body after the Sun. Its unique position, as partner to the Earth on its journey around the solar system, means that the Moon appears to pass through the signs of the zodiac extremely quickly. The zodiac position of the Moon at the time of your birth plays a great part in personal character and is especially significant in the build-up of your emotional nature.

Your Own Moon Sign

Discovering the position of the Moon at the time of your birth has always been notoriously difficult because tracking the complex zodiac positions of the Moon is not easy. This process has been reduced to three simple stages with our Lunar Tables. A breakdown of the Moon's zodiac positions can be found from page 35 onwards, so that once you know what your Moon Sign is, you can see what part this plays in the overall build-up of your personal character.

If you follow the instructions on the next page you will soon be able to work out exactly what zodiac sign the Moon occupied on the day that you were born and you can then go on to compare the reading for this position with those of your Sun sign and your Ascendant. It is partly the comparison between these three important positions that goes towards making you the unique individual you are.

HOW TO DISCOVER YOUR MOON SIGN

This is a three-stage process. You may need a pen and a piece of paper but if you follow the instructions below the process should only take a minute or so.

STAGE 1 First of all you need to know the Moon Age at the time of your birth. If you look at Moon Table 1, on page 33, you will find all the years between 1919 and 2017 down the left side. Find the year of your birth and then trace across to the right to the month of your birth. Where the two intersect you will find a number. This is the date of the New Moon in the month that you were born. You now need to count forward the number of days between the New Moon and your own birthday. For example, if the New Moon in the month of your birth was shown as being the 6th and you were born on the 20th, your Moon Age Day would be 14. If the New Moon in the month of your birth came after your birthday, you need to count forward from the New Moon in the previous month. Whatever the result, jot this number down so that you do not forget it.

STAGE 2 Take a look at Moon Table 2 on page 34. Down the left hand column look for the date of your birth. Now trace across to the month of your birth. Where the two meet you will find a letter. Copy this letter down alongside your Moon Age Day.

STAGE 3 Moon Table 3 on page 34 will supply you with the zodiac sign the Moon occupied on the day of your birth. Look for your Moon Age Day down the left hand column and then for the letter you found in Stage 2. Where the two converge you will find a zodiac sign and this is the sign occupied by the Moon on the day that you were born.

Your Zodiac Moon Sign Explained

You will find a profile of all zodiac Moon Signs on pages 35 to 38, showing in yet another way how astrology helps to make you into the individual that you are. In each daily entry of the Astral Diary you can find the zodiac position of the Moon for every day of the year. This also allows you to discover your lunar birthdays. Since the Moon passes through all the signs of the zodiac in about a month, you can expect something like twelve lunar birthdays each year. At these times you are likely to be emotionally steady and able to make the sort of decisions that have real, lasting value.

MOON TABLE 1

YEAR	SEP	OCT	NOV	YEAR	SEP	OCT	NOV	YEAR	SEP	OCT	NOV
1919	23	23	22	1952	19	18	17	1985	14	14	12
1920	12	12	10	1953	8	8	6	1986	4	3	2
1921	2	1/30	29	1954	27	26	25	1987	23	22	21
1922	21	20	19	1955	16	15	14	1988	11	10	9
1923	10	10	8	1956	4	4	2	1989	29	29	28
1924	28	28	26	1957	23	23	21	1990	19	18	17
1925	18	17	16	1958	13	12	11	1991	8	8	6
1926	7	6	5	1959	3	2/31	30	1992	26	25	24
1927	25	25	24	1960	21	20	19	1993	16	15	14
1928	14	14	12	1961	10	9	8	1994	5	5	3
1929	3	2	1	1962	28	28	27	1995	24	24	22
1930	22	20	19	1963	17	17	15	1996	13	11	10
1931	12	11	9	1964	6	5	4	1997	2	2/31	30
1932	30	29	27	1965	25	24	22	1998	20	20	19
1933	19	19	17	1966	14	14	12	1999	9	9	8
1934	9	8	7	1967	4	3	2	2000	27	27	26
1935	27	27	26	1968	23	22	21	2001	17	17	16
1936	15	15	14	1969	11	10	9	2002	6	6	4
1937	4	4	3	1970	1	1/30	29	2003	26	25	24
1938	23	23	22	1971	19	19	18	2004	13	12	11
1939	13	12	11	1972	8	8	6	2005	3	2	1
1940	2	1/30	29	1973	27	26	25	2006	22	21	20
1941	21	20	19	1974	16	15	14	2007	12	11	9
1942	10	10	8	1975	5	5	3	2008	30	29	28
1943	29	29	27	1976	23	23	21	2009	19	18	17
1944	17	17	15	1977	13	12	11	2010	8	8	6
1945	6	6	4	1978	2	2/31	30	2011	27	27	25
1946	25	24	23	1979	21	20	19	2012	6	15	13
1947	14	14	12	1980	10	9	8	2013	4	4	2
1948	3	2	1	1981	28	27	26	2014	23	22	22
1949	23	21	20	1982	17	17	15	2015	13	12	11
1950	12	11	9	1983	7	6	4	2016	1	30	29
1951	1	1/30	29	1984	25	24	22	2017	20	20	18

TABLE 2   MOON TABLE 3

DAY	OCT	NOV	M/D	a	b	d	e	f	g	i
1	a	e	0	LI	LI	LI	SC	SC	SC	SA
2	a	e	1	LI	LI	SC	SC	SC	SA	SA
3	a	e	2	LI	SC	SC	SC	SA	SA	CP
4	b	f	3	SC	SC	SC	SA	SA	CP	CP
5	b	f	4	SC	SA	SA	SA	CP	CP	CP
6	b	f	5	SA	SA	SA	CP	CP	AQ	AQ
7	b	f	6	SA	CP	CP	CP	AQ	AQ	AQ
8	b	f	7	SA	CP	CP	AQ	AQ	PI	PI
9	b	f	8	CP	CP	CP	AQ	PI	PI	PI
10	b	f	9	CP	AQ	AQ	AQ	PI	PI	AR
11	b	f	10	AQ	AQ	AQ	PI	AR	AR	AR
12	b	f	11	AQ	PI	PI	PI	AR	AR	TA
13	b	g	12	PI	PI	PI	AR	TA	TA	TA
14	d	g	13	PI	AR	PI	AR	TA	TA	GE
15	d	g	14	AR	AR	AR	TA	GE	GE	GE
16	d	g	15	AR	AR	AR	TA	TA	TA	GE
17	d	g	16	AR	AR	TA	TA	GE	GE	GE
18	d	g	17	AR	TA	TA	GE	GE	GE	CA
19	d	g	18	TA	TA	GE	GE	GE	CA	CA
20	d	g	19	TA	TA	GE	GE	CA	CA	CA
21	d	g	20	GE	GE	GE	CA	CA	CA	LE
22	d	g	21	GE	GE	CA	CA	CA	LE	LE
23	d	i	22	GE	CA	CA	CA	LE	LE	VI
24	e	i	23	CA	CA	CA	LE	LE	LE	VI
25	e	i	24	CA	CA	LE	LE	LE	VI	VI
26	e	i	25	CA	LE	LE	LE	VI	VI	LI
27	e	i	26	LE	LE	VI	VI	VI	LI	LI
28	e	i	27	LE	VI	VI	VI	LI	LI	SC
29	e	i	28	VI	VI	VI	LI	LI	LI	SC
30	e	i	29	VI	VI	LI	LI	LI	SC	SC
31	e	–								

AR = Aries, TA = Taurus, GE = Gemini, CA = Cancer, LE = Leo, VI = Virgo,
LI = Libra, SC = Scorpio, SA = Sagittarius, CP = Capricorn, AQ = Aquarius, PI = Pisces

MOON SIGNS

Moon in Aries

You have a strong imagination, courage, determination and a desire to do things in your own way and forge your own path through life.

Originality is a key attribute; you are seldom stuck for ideas although your mind is changeable and you could take the time to focus on individual tasks. Often quick-tempered, you take orders from few people and live life at a fast pace. Avoid health problems by taking regular time out for rest and relaxation.

Emotionally, it is important that you talk to those you are closest to and work out your true feelings. Once you discover that people are there to help, there is less necessity for you to do everything yourself.

Moon in Taurus

The Moon in Taurus gives you a courteous and friendly manner, which means you are likely to have many friends.

The good things in life mean a lot to you, as Taurus is an Earth sign that delights in experiences which please the senses. Hence you are probably a lover of good food and drink, which may in turn mean you need to keep an eye on the bathroom scales, especially as looking good is also important to you.

Emotionally you are fairly stable and you stick by your own standards. Taureans do not respond well to change. Intuition also plays an important part in your life.

Moon in Gemini

You have a warm-hearted character, sympathetic and eager to help others. At times reserved, you can also be articulate and chatty: this is part of the paradox of Gemini, which always brings duplicity to the nature. You are interested in current affairs, have a good intellect, and are good company and likely to have many friends. Most of your friends have a high opinion of you and would be ready to defend you should the need arise. However, this is usually unnecessary, as you are quite capable of defending yourself in any verbal confrontation.

Travel is important to your inquisitive mind and you find intellectual stimulus in mixing with people from different cultures. You also gain much from reading, writing and the arts but you do need plenty of rest and relaxation in order to avoid fatigue.

Moon in Cancer

The Moon in Cancer at the time of birth is a fortunate position as Cancer is the Moon's natural home. This means that the qualities of compassion and understanding given by the Moon are especially enhanced in your nature, and you are friendly and sociable and cope well with emotional pressures. You cherish home and family life, and happily do the domestic tasks. Your surroundings are important to you and you hate squalor and filth. You are likely to have a love of music and poetry.

Your basic character, although at times changeable like the Moon itself, depends on symmetry. You aim to make your surroundings comfortable and harmonious, for yourself and those close to you.

Moon in Leo

The best qualities of the Moon and Leo come together to make you warm-hearted, fair, ambitious and self-confident. With good organisational abilities, you invariably rise to a position of responsibility in your chosen career. This is fortunate as you don't enjoy being an 'also-ran' and would rather be an important part of a small organisation than a menial in a large one.

You should be lucky in love and happy, provided you put in the effort to make a comfortable home for yourself and those close to you. It is likely that you will have a love of pleasure, sport, music and literature. Life brings you many rewards, most of them as a direct result of your own efforts, although you may be luckier than average and ready to make the best of any situation.

Moon in Virgo

You are endowed with good mental abilities and a keen receptive memory, but you are never ostentatious or pretentious. Naturally quite reserved, you still have many friends, especially of the opposite sex. Marital relationships must be discussed carefully and worked at so that they remain harmonious, as personal attachments can be a problem if you do not give them your full attention.

Talented and persevering, you possess artistic qualities and are a good homemaker. Earning your honours through genuine merit, you work long and hard towards your objectives but show little pride in your achievements. Many short journeys will be undertaken in your life.

Moon in Libra

With the Moon in Libra you are naturally popular and make friends easily. People like you, probably more than you realise, you bring fun to a party and are a natural diplomat. For all its good points, Libra is not the most stable of astrological signs and, as a result, your emotions can be a little unstable too. Therefore, although the Moon in Libra is said to be good for love and marriage, your Sun sign and Rising sign will have an important effect on your emotional and loving qualities.

You must remember to relate to others in your decision-making. Co-operation is crucial because Libra represents the 'balance' of life that can only be achieved through harmonious relationships. Conformity is not easy for you because Libra, an Air sign, likes its independence.

Moon in Scorpio

Some people might call you pushy. In fact, all you really want to do is to live life to the full and protect yourself and your family from the pressures of life. Take care to avoid giving the impression of being sarcastic or impulsive and use your energies wisely and constructively.

You have great courage and you invariably achieve your goals by force of personality and sheer effort. You are fond of mystery and are good at predicting the outcome of situations and events. Travel experiences can be beneficial to you.

You may experience problems if you do not take time to examine your motives in a relationship, and also if you allow jealousy, always a feature of Scorpio, to cloud your judgement.

Moon in Sagittarius

The Moon in Sagittarius helps to make you a generous individual with humanitarian qualities and a kind heart. Restlessness may be intrinsic as your mind is seldom still. Perhaps because of this, you have a need for change that could lead you to several major moves during your adult life. You are not afraid to stand your ground when you know your judgement is right, you speak directly and have good intuition.

At work you are quick, efficient and versatile and so you make an ideal employee. You need work to be intellectually demanding and do not enjoy tedious routines.

In relationships, you anger quickly if faced with stupidity or deception, though you are just as quick to forgive and forget. Emotionally, there are times when your heart rules your head.

Moon in Capricorn

The Moon in Capricorn makes you popular and likely to come into the public eye in some way. The watery Moon is not entirely comfortable in the Earth sign of Capricorn and this may lead to some difficulties in the early years of life. An initial lack of creative ability and indecision must be overcome before the true qualities of patience and perseverance inherent in Capricorn can show through.

You have good administrative ability and are a capable worker, and if you are careful you can accumulate wealth. But you must be cautious and take professional advice in partnerships, as you are open to deception. You may be interested in social or welfare work, which suit your organisational skills and sympathy for others.

Moon in Aquarius

The Moon in Aquarius makes you an active and agreeable person with a friendly, easy-going nature. Sympathetic to the needs of others, you flourish in a laid-back atmosphere. You are broad-minded, fair and open to suggestion, although sometimes you have an unconventional quality which others can find hard to understand.

You are interested in the strange and curious, and in old articles and places. You enjoy trips to these places and gain much from them. Political, scientific and educational work interests you and you might choose a career in science or technology.

Money-wise, you make gains through innovation and concentration and Lunar Aquarians often tackle more than one job at a time. In love you are kind and honest.

Moon in Pisces

You have a kind, sympathetic nature, somewhat retiring at times, but you always take account of others' feelings and help when you can.

Personal relationships may be problematic, but as life goes on you can learn from your experiences and develop a better understanding of yourself and the world around you.

You have a fondness for travel, appreciate beauty and harmony and hate disorder and strife. You may be fond of literature and would make a good writer or speaker yourself. You have a creative imagination and may come across as an incurable romantic. You have strong intuition, maybe bordering on a mediumistic quality, which sets you apart from the mass. You may not be rich in cash terms, but your personal gifts are worth more than gold.

SCORPIO IN LOVE

Discover how compatible you are with people from the same and other parts of the zodiac. Five stars equals a match made in heaven!

Scorpio meets Scorpio

Scorpio is deep, complex and enigmatic, traits which often lead to misunderstanding with other zodiac signs, so a double Scorpio match can work well because both parties understand one another. They will allow each other periods of silence and reflection but still be willing to help, advise and support when necessary. Their relationship may seem odd to others but that doesn't matter if those involved are happy. All in all, an unusual but contented combination. Star rating: *****

Scorpio meets Sagittarius

Sagittarius needs constant stimulation and loves to be busy from dawn till dusk which may mean that it feels rather frustrated by Scorpio. Scorpions are hard workers, too, but they are also contemplative and need periods of quiet which may mean that they appear dull to Sagittarius. This could lead to a gulf between the two which must be overcome. With time and patience on both sides, this can be a lucrative encounter and good in terms of home and family. A variable alliance. Star rating: ***

Scorpio meets Capricorn

Lack of communication is the governing factor here. Neither of this pair are renowned communicators and both need a partner to draw out their full verbal potential. Consequently, Scorpio may find Capricorn cold and unapproachable while Capricorn could find Scorpio dark and brooding. Both are naturally tidy and would keep a pristine house but great effort and a mutual goal is needed on both sides to overcome the missing spark. A good match on the financial side, but probably not an earth-shattering personal encounter. Star rating: **

Scorpio meets Aquarius

This is a promising and practical combination. Scorpio responds well to Aquarius' exploration of its deep nature and so this shy sign becomes lighter, brighter and more inspirational. Meanwhile, Aquarians are rarely as sure of themselves as they like to appear and are reassured by Scorpio's steady and determined support. Both signs want to be kind to the other which is a basis for a relationship that should be warm most of the time and extremely hot occasionally. Star rating: ****

Scorpio meets Pisces

If ever there were two zodiac signs that have a total rapport, it has to be Scorpio and Pisces. They share very similar needs: they are not gregarious and are happy with a little silence, good music and time to contemplate the finer things in life, and both are attracted to family life. Apart, they can have a tendency to wander in a romantic sense, but this is reduced when they come together. They are deep, firm friends who enjoy each other's company and this must lead to an excellent chance of success. These people are surely made for each other! Star rating: *****

Scorpio meets Aries

There can be great affection here, even if the two signs are so very different. The common link is the planet Mars, which plays a part in both these natures. Although Aries is, outwardly, the most dominant, Scorpio people are among the most powerful to be found anywhere. This quiet determination is respected by Aries. Aries will satisfy the passionate side of Scorpio, particularly with instruction from Scorpio. There are mysteries here which will add spice to life. The few arguments that do occur are likely to be awe-inspiring. Star rating: ****

Scorpio meets Taurus

Scorpio is deep – very deep – which may be a problem, because Taurus doesn't wear its heart on its sleeve either. It might be difficult for this pair to get together, because neither is naturally inclined to make the first move. Taurus stands in awe of the power and intensity of the Scorpio mind, while the Scorpion is interested in the Bull's affable and friendly qualities, so an enduring relationship could be forged if the couple ever get round to talking. Both are lovers of home and family, which will help to cement a relationship. Star rating: **

Scorpio meets Gemini

There could be problems here. Scorpio is one of the deepest and least understood of all the zodiac signs, which at first seems like a challenge to intellectual Gemini, who thinks it can solve anything. But the deeper the Gemini digs, the further down Scorpio goes. Meanwhile, Scorpio may be finding Gemini thoughtless, shallow and even downright annoying. Gemini is often afraid of Scorpio's perception and strength, together with the sting in the Scorpion's tail. Anything is possible, but the outlook for this match is less than promising. Star rating: **

Scorpio meets Cancer

This match is potentially a great success, a fact which is often a mystery to astrologers. Some feel it is due to the compatibility of the Water element, but it could also come from a mixture of similarity and difference in the personalities. Scorpio is partly ruled by Mars, which gives it a deep, passionate, dominant and powerful side. Cancerians generally like and respect this amalgam, and recognise something there that they would like to adopt themselves. On the other side of the coin, Scorpio needs love and emotional security which Cancer offers generously. Star rating: *****

Scorpio meets Leo

Stand back and watch the sparks fly! Scorpio has the deep sensitivity of a Water sign but it is also partially ruled by Fire planet Mars, from which it draws great power, and Leo will find that difficult. Leo loves to take charge and really hates to feel psychologically undermined, which is Scorpio's stock-in-trade. Scorpio may find Leo's ideals a little shallow, which will be upsetting to the Lion. Anything is possible, but this possibility is rather slimmer than most. Star rating: **

Scorpio meets Virgo

There are one or two potential difficulties here, but there is also a meeting point from which to overcome them. Virgo is very caring and protective, a trait which Scorpio understands and even emulates. Scorpio will impress Virgo with its serious side. Both signs are consistent, although also sarcastic. Scorpio may uncover a hidden passion in Virgo which all too often lies deep within its Earth-sign nature. Material success is very likely, with Virgo taking the lion's share of the domestic chores and family responsibilities. Star rating: ***

Scorpio meets Libra

Many astrologers have reservations about this match because, on the surface, the signs are so different. However, this couple may find fulfilment because these differences mean that their respective needs are met. Scorpio needs a partner to lighten the load, which won't daunt Libra, while Libra looks for a steadfast quality which it doesn't possess, but which Scorpio can supply naturally. Financial success is possible because they both have good ideas and back them up with hard work and determination. All in all, a promising outlook. Star rating: ****

VENUS:
THE PLANET OF LOVE

If you look up at the sky around sunset or sunrise you will often see Venus in close attendance to the Sun. It is arguably one of the most beautiful sights of all and there is little wonder that historically it became associated with the goddess of love. But although Venus does play an important part in the way you view love and in the way others see you romantically, this is only one of the spheres of influence that it enjoys in your overall character.

Venus has a part to play in the more cultured side of your life and has much to do with your appreciation of art, literature, music and general creativity. Even the way you look is responsive to the part of the zodiac that Venus occupied at the start of your life, though this fact is also down to your Sun sign and Ascending sign. If, at the time you were born, Venus occupied one of the more gregarious zodiac signs, you will be more likely to wear your heart on your sleeve, as well as to be more attracted to entertainment, social gatherings and good company. If on the other hand Venus occupied a quiet zodiac sign at the time of your birth, you would tend to be more retiring and less willing to shine in public situations.

It's good to know what part the planet Venus plays in your life for it can have a great bearing on the way you appear to the rest of the world and since we all have to mix with others, you can learn to make the very best of what Venus has to offer you.

One of the great complications in the past has always been trying to establish exactly what zodiac position Venus enjoyed when you were born because the planet is notoriously difficult to track. However, we have solved that problem by creating a table that is exclusive to your Sun sign, which you will find on the following page.

Establishing your Venus sign could not be easier. Just look up the year of your birth on the next page and you will see a sign of the zodiac. This was the sign that Venus occupied in the period covered by your sign in that year. If Venus occupied more than one sign during the period, this is indicated by the date on which the sign changed, and the name of the new sign. For instance, if you were born in 1950, Venus was in Libra until the 28th October, after which time it was in Scorpio. If you were born before 28th October your Venus sign is Libra, if you were born on or after 28th October, your Venus sign is Scorpio. Once you have established the position of Venus at the time of your birth, you can then look in the pages which follow to see how this has a bearing on your life as a whole.

1919 VIRGO / 9.11 LIBRA
1920 SCORPIO / 24.10 SAGITTARIUS /
17.11 CAPRICORN
1921 LIBRA / 14.11 SCORPIO
1922 SAGITTARIUS / 16.11 SCORPIO
1923 SCORPIO / 9.11 SAGITTARIUS
1924 VIRGO / 3.11 LIBRA
1925 SAGITTARIUS / 7.11 CAPRICORN
1926 LIBRA / 29.10 SCORPIO
1927 VIRGO / 10.11 LIBRA
1928 SAGITTARIUS /
17.11 CAPRICORN
1929 LIBRA / 13.11 SCORPIO
1930 SAGITTARIUS / 16.11 SCORPIO
1931 SCORPIO / 8.11 SAGITTARIUS
1932 VIRGO / 2.11 LIBRA
1933 SAGITTARIUS / 7.11 CAPRICORN
1934 LIBRA / 29.10 SCORPIO
1935 VIRGO / 10.11 LIBRA
1936 SAGITTARIUS /
16.11 CAPRICORN
1937 LIBRA / 13.11 SCORPIO
1938 SAGITTARIUS / 16.11 SCORPIO
1939 SCORPIO / 7.11 SAGITTARIUS
1940 VIRGO / 2.11 LIBRA
1941 SAGITTARIUS / 7.11 CAPRICORN
1942 LIBRA / 28.10 SCORPIO
1943 VIRGO / 10.11 LIBRA
1944 SAGITTARIUS /
16.11 CAPRICORN
1945 LIBRA / 13.11 SCORPIO
1946 SAGITTARIUS / 16.11 SCORPIO
1947 SCORPIO / 6.11 SAGITTARIUS
1948 VIRGO / 1.11 LIBRA
1949 SAGITTARIUS / 6.11 CAPRICORN
1950 LIBRA / 28.10 SCORPIO
1951 VIRGO / 10.11 LIBRA
1952 SAGITTARIUS /
16.11 CAPRICORN
1953 LIBRA / 12.11 SCORPIO
1954 SAGITTARIUS / 28.10 SCORPIO
1955 SCORPIO / 6.11 SAGITTARIUS
1956 VIRGO / 1.11 LIBRA
1957 SAGITTARIUS / 6.11 CAPRICORN
1958 LIBRA / 27.10 SCORPIO
1959 VIRGO / 10.11 LIBRA
1960 SAGITTARIUS /
15.11 CAPRICORN
1961 LIBRA / 12.11 SCORPIO
1962 SAGITTARIUS / 28.10 SCORPIO
1963 SCORPIO / 5.11 SAGITTARIUS
1964 VIRGO / 31.10 LIBRA
1965 SAGITTARIUS / 6.11 CAPRICORN
1966 LIBRA / 27.10 SCORPIO
1967 VIRGO / 10.11 LIBRA
1968 SAGITTARIUS /

15.11 CAPRICORN
1969 LIBRA / 11.11 SCORPIO
1970 SAGITTARIUS / 28.10 SCORPIO
1971 SCORPIO / 4.11 SAGITTARIUS
1972 VIRGO / 31.10 LIBRA
1973 SAGITTARIUS / 6.11 CAPRICORN
1974 LIBRA / 26.10 SCORPIO
1975 VIRGO / 9.11 LIBRA
1976 SAGITTARIUS /
15.11 CAPRICORN
1977 LIBRA / 11.11 SCORPIO
1978 SAGITTARIUS / 28.10 SCORPIO
1979 SCORPIO / 4.11 SAGITTARIUS
1980 VIRGO / 30.10 LIBRA
1981 SAGITTARIUS / 5.11 CAPRICORN
1982 LIBRA / 26.10 SCORPIO
1983 VIRGO / 9.11 LIBRA
1984 SAGITTARIUS /
14.11 CAPRICORN
1985 LIBRA / 10.11 SCORPIO
1986 SAGITTARIUS / 28.10 SCORPIO
1987 SCORPIO / 3.11 SAGITTARIUS
1988 VIRGO / 30.10 LIBRA
1989 SAGITTARIUS / 5.11 CAPRICORN
1990 LIBRA / 25.10 SCORPIO
1991 VIRGO / 9.11 LIBRA
1992 SAGITTARIUS /
14.11 CAPRICORN
1993 LIBRA / 10.11 SCORPIO
1994 SAGITTARIUS / 28.10 SCORPIO
1995 SCORPIO / 3.11 SAGITTARIUS
1996 VIRGO / 29.10 LIBRA
1997 SAGITTARIUS / 5.11 CAPRICORN
1998 LIBRA / 25.10 SCORPIO
1999 VIRGO / 9.11 LIBRA
2000 SAGITTARIUS /
14.11 CAPRICORN
2001 LIBRA / 10.11 SCORPIO
2002 SAGITTARIUS / 28.10 SCORPIO
2003 SCORPIO / 3.11 SAGITTARIUS
2004 VIRGO / 29.10 LIBRA
2005 SAGITTARIUS / 5.11 CAPRICORN
2006 LIBRA / 25.10 SCORPIO
2007 VIRGO / 9.11 LIBRA
2008 SAGITTARIUS /
14.11 CAPRICORN
2009 LIBRA / 10.11 SCORPIO
2010 SAGITTARIUS / 28.10 SCORPIO
2011 SCORPIO / 3.11 SAGITTARIUS
2012 VIRGO / 29.10 LIBRA
2013 SAGITTARIUS / 5.11 CAPRICORN
2014 LIBRA / 25.10 SCORPIO
2015 VIRGO / 9.11 LIBRA
2016 SAGITTARIUS /
13.11 CAPRICORN
2017 LIBRA / 10.11 SCORPIO

VENUS THROUGH THE ZODIAC SIGNS

Venus in Aries

Amongst other things, the position of Venus in Aries indicates a fondness for travel, music and all creative pursuits. Your nature tends to be affectionate and you would try not to create confusion or difficulty for others if it could be avoided. Many people with this planetary position have a great love of the theatre, and mental stimulation is of the greatest importance. Early romantic attachments are common with Venus in Aries, so it is very important to establish a genuine sense of romantic continuity. Early marriage is not recommended, especially if it is based on sympathy. You may give your heart a little too readily on occasions.

Venus in Taurus

You are capable of very deep feelings and your emotions tend to last for a very long time. This makes you a trusting partner and lover, whose constancy is second to none. In life you are precise and careful and always try to do things the right way. Although this means an ordered life, which you are comfortable with, it can also lead you to be rather too fussy for your own good. Despite your pleasant nature, you are very fixed in your opinions and quite able to speak your mind. Others are attracted to you and historical astrologers always quoted this position of Venus as being very fortunate in terms of marriage. However, if you find yourself involved in a failed relationship, it could take you a long time to trust again.

Venus in Gemini

As with all associations related to Gemini, you tend to be quite versatile, anxious for change and intelligent in your dealings with the world at large. You may gain money from more than one source but you are equally good at spending it. There is an inference here that you are a good communicator, via either the written or the spoken word, and you love to be in the company of interesting people. Always on the look-out for culture, you may also be very fond of music, and love to indulge the curious and cultured side of your nature. In romance you tend to have more than one relationship and could find yourself associated with someone who has previously been a friend or even a distant relative.

Venus in Cancer

You often stay close to home because you are very fond of family and enjoy many of your most treasured moments when you are with those you love. Being naturally sympathetic, you will always do anything you can to support those around you, even people you hardly know at all. This charitable side of your nature is your most noticeable trait and is one of the reasons why others are naturally so fond of you. Being receptive and in some cases even psychic, you can see through to the soul of most of those with whom you come into contact. You may not commence too many romantic attachments but when you do give your heart, it tends to be unconditionally.

Venus in Leo

It must become quickly obvious to almost anyone you meet that you are kind, sympathetic and yet determined enough to stand up for anyone or anything that is truly important to you. Bright and sunny, you warm the world with your natural enthusiasm and would rarely do anything to hurt those around you, or at least not intentionally. In romance you are ardent and sincere, though some may find your style just a little overpowering. Gains come through your contacts with other people and this could be especially true with regard to romance, for love and money often come hand in hand for those who were born with Venus in Leo. People claim to understand you, though you are more complex than you seem.

Venus in Virgo

Your nature could well be fairly quiet no matter what your Sun sign might be, though this fact often manifests itself as an inner peace and would not prevent you from being basically sociable. Some delays and even the odd disappointment in love cannot be ruled out with this planetary position, though it's a fact that you will usually find the happiness you look for in the end. Catapulting yourself into romantic entanglements that you know to be rather ill-advised is not sensible, and it would be better to wait before you committed yourself exclusively to any one person. It is the essence of your nature to serve the world at large and through doing so it is possible that you will attract money at some stage in your life.

Venus in Libra

Venus is very comfortable in Libra and bestows upon those people who have this planetary position a particular sort of kindness that is easy to recognise. This is a very good position for all sorts of friendships and also for romantic attachments that usually bring much joy into your life. Few individuals with Venus in Libra would avoid marriage and since you are capable of great depths of love, it is likely that you will find a contented personal life. You like to mix with people of integrity and intelligence but don't take kindly to scruffy surroundings or work that means getting your hands too dirty. Careful speculation, good business dealings and money through marriage all seem fairly likely.

Venus in Scorpio

You are quite open and tend to spend money quite freely, even on those occasions when you don't have very much. Although your intentions are always good, there are times when you get yourself in to the odd scrape and this can be particularly true when it comes to romance, which you may come to late or from a rather unexpected direction. Certainly you have the power to be happy and to make others contented on the way, but you find the odd stumbling block on your journey through life and it could seem that you have to work harder than those around you. As a result of this, you gain a much deeper understanding of the true value of personal happiness than many people ever do, and are likely to achieve true contentment in the end.

Venus in Sagittarius

You are lighthearted, cheerful and always able to see the funny side of any situation. These facts enhance your popularity, which is especially high with members of the opposite sex. You should never have to look too far to find romantic interest in your life, though it is just possible that you might be too willing to commit yourself before you are certain that the person in question is right for you. Part of the problem here extends to other areas of life too. The fact is that you like variety in everything and so can tire of situations that fail to offer it. All the same, if you choose wisely and learn to understand your restless side, then great happiness can be yours.

Venus in Capricorn

The most notable trait that comes from Venus in this position is that it makes you trustworthy and able to take on all sorts of responsibilities in life. People are instinctively fond of you and love you all the more because you are always ready to help those who are in any form of need. Social and business popularity can be yours and there is a magnetic quality to your nature that is particularly attractive in a romantic sense. Anyone who wants a partner for a lover, a spouse and a good friend too would almost certainly look in your direction. Constancy is the hallmark of your nature and unfaithfulness would go right against the grain. You might sometimes be a little too trusting.

Venus in Aquarius

This location of Venus offers a fondness for travel and a desire to try out something new at every possible opportunity. You are extremely easy to get along with and tend to have many friends from varied backgrounds, classes and inclinations. You like to live a distinct sort of life and gain a great deal from moving about, both in a career sense and with regard to your home. It is not out of the question that you could form a romantic attachment to someone who comes from far away or be attracted to a person of a distinctly artistic and original nature. What you cannot stand is jealousy, for you have friends of both sexes and would want to keep things that way.

Venus in Pisces

The first thing people tend to notice about you is your wonderful, warm smile. Being very charitable by nature you will do anything to help others, even if you don't know them well. Much of your life may be spent sorting out situations for other people, but it is very important to feel that you are living for yourself too. In the main, you remain cheerful, and tend to be quite attractive to members of the opposite sex. Where romantic attachments are concerned, you could be drawn to people who are significantly older or younger than yourself or to someone with a unique career or point of view. It might be best for you to avoid marrying whilst you are still very young.

SCORPIO:
2016 DIARY PAGES

October
2016

1 SATURDAY
Moon Age Day 1   Moon Sign Libra

Your home today seems to be a refuge from the pressures that may be building up in the outside world. There are times when it is absolutely necessary for Scorpio to stand still and take stock. You are entering one of these periods and it will do you no harm at all to take a few hours to be with those you love.

2 SUNDAY
Moon Age Day 2   Moon Sign Libra

Don't expect to move too many mountains today but be content with sorting out those little important details. It would be useful to take this time ahead of the lunar high to review your recent efforts, and focus your mind with determination to clear obstacles from your path. This is a day of preparation rather than direct action.

3 MONDAY
Moon Age Day 3   Moon Sign Scorpio

It is now your monthly lunar high, a time during which your powers of influence are at their strongest. If there is anything you really want, now is the right time to go out and ask for it. New strategies work well and you are on the ball socially. Most importantly, your popularity knows no bounds.

4 TUESDAY
Moon Age Day 4   Moon Sign Scorpio

You get the maximum reward for your efforts today and Lady Luck is likely to be on your side. This means being willing to take the odd chance, something you are less than willing to do as a rule. You will also be very physically motivated and maybe inclined to take on new sporting activities.

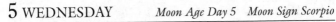

5 WEDNESDAY   *Moon Age Day 5   Moon Sign Scorpio*

Both your popularity and your ego are likely to be extremely strong at the moment, but there is just a slight possibility that you are not taking the needs and desires of others into account as much as would usually be the case. This is unusual for you but is something that deserves extra attention.

6 THURSDAY   *Moon Age Day 6   Moon Sign Sagittarius*

You show an appealing and happy-go-lucky approach to many aspects of life and this ensures that you remain popular when in company. Whether you are as pleased with yourself as others seem to be with you remains in some doubt. There is often a burning desire within you to do better and this really shows now.

7 FRIDAY   *Moon Age Day 7   Moon Sign Sagittarius*

Professional developments are on the cards and you are in one of the most practical phases of the month. Where you might have had some difficulty in the recent past you now show yourself to be equal to almost any task. All the same, don't take on too much and address situations one at a time today.

8 SATURDAY   *Moon Age Day 8   Moon Sign Capricorn*

Don't expect everything to be totally stable this weekend. You reveal a tendency to go down some fairly abortive paths when it comes to practical matters and may need to think again about certain projects or ideas. Take some time out to enjoy what the weekend has to offer in a social sense.

9 SUNDAY   *Moon Age Day 9   Moon Sign Capricorn*

You should now be going for your major objectives in life with great gusto and what really sets you apart at the moment is that you will not take no for an answer. Certain people will be surprised at your attitude because you don't often show this forceful side. Maybe being pulled up in their tracks will do them good, however.

10 MONDAY *Moon Age Day 10   Moon Sign Capricorn*

If you really want to get on well at the start of this week you are going to have to inspire a more gregarious and happy-go-lucky attitude than the one that is naturally a part of your personality. The effort will be worthwhile, if only because you make such a good impression on people who could just be in a position to help you.

11 TUESDAY *Moon Age Day 11   Moon Sign Aquarius*

Concentration is necessary today if you are not to allow something important to slip through your fingers. It won't always be easy to remain patient with people who appear determined to be stupid, but being a Scorpio you will manage somehow. By the evening you could be quite happy to settle for a happy social event.

12 WEDNESDAY *Moon Age Day 12   Moon Sign Aquarius*

Today you show good general self-awareness and a shrewd mind that is not likely to be fooled by anyone. You are also getting far more determined. Once you have made up your mind to follow a particular course of action, all the king's horses and all the king's men won't divert you from it.

13 THURSDAY *Moon Age Day 13   Moon Sign Pisces*

Expressing yourself has probably never been more fun than it appears to be right now. Don't be too quick to criticise the actions of another, especially bearing in mind that they may only be trying to follow your lead. All in all you should be fairly happy with your lot today and things get much busier tomorrow.

14 FRIDAY *Moon Age Day 14   Moon Sign Pisces*

Communication remains the key to success. Talk, talk and more talk is the order of the day and if you don't get involved in discussions at all levels you could lose out. Even when you must deal with people you don't especially care for it is possible to achieve a consensus of opinion at the moment.

15 SATURDAY   *Moon Age Day 15   Moon Sign Aries*

This is still a very beneficial period when it comes to forward planning but there are also some very strong social trends around. For these reasons you may be carefully splitting your day between those matters that are of a practical nature and times when you simply intend to have a good time.

16 SUNDAY   *Moon Age Day 16   Moon Sign Aries*

You are likely to be feeling good about yourself but you display this in a fairly quiet way. Whilst others may boast, you remain calm and simply get on with things. The knowledge that you know where you are going and that you are fully conversant regarding the way you will deal with life can be quite satisfying.

17 MONDAY   *Moon Age Day 17   Moon Sign Taurus*

You should find today to be fairly quiet and although that means that you may not make some of the progress you might wish, you can at least relax a little. The lunar low this time around is not likely to prove particularly stressful, even if it does cause you to be slightly less approachable than of late.

18 TUESDAY   *Moon Age Day 18   Moon Sign Taurus*

You will still be spending at least part of today in that deep and unfathomable world of your own. When Scorpio retreats into itself, nobody can follow. Make a point of letting people know that there is nothing fundamentally wrong with you and that you just need space and time to reflect on life.

19 WEDNESDAY   *Moon Age Day 19   Moon Sign Gemini*

Today you really will experience life at an emotional level. Intuition is strong and can guide you accurately when it comes to making the right decisions but you are hardly as practical as would often be the case. As the day wears on you should register the fact that you are becoming more vocal, especially with friends.

20 THURSDAY
Moon Age Day 20   Moon Sign Gemini

What seemed like a sound and practical idea at the time is now less appealing and you could find that you are working very hard to no real end. One fact about Scorpio that is always present is your resistance to giving in and though this is usually a laudable quality it might mean even more toil for nothing now.

21 FRIDAY
Moon Age Day 21   Moon Sign Cancer

What you hear from colleagues and friends now might throw some light on to a mystery from the past. Try to reach out to people in different walks of life and learn from what they have to say. You are gradually climbing into a much stronger personal position and will be getting back some of that earlier optimism.

22 SATURDAY
Moon Age Day 22   Moon Sign Cancer

This would be a good day to do something recreational. At the same time you are being quite creative and can expect an end product from all your efforts. On a slightly negative note, you need to be careful about what you say in open discussions. It is quite possible to give offence without intending to do so.

23 SUNDAY
Moon Age Day 23   Moon Sign Leo

You might need some help today but it is not likely to be very far away. You should also find moments for quiet reflection, which is necessary if the actions you are going to take are well thought out and considered. Allow family members a little more leeway than might have been the case recently.

24 MONDAY
Moon Age Day 24   Moon Sign Leo

Your natural sense of compassion now makes you anxious to help those who are less well off than you are. This is also a good time to be with friends but this is not a particularly useful period for inviting strangers into your life. You are still not firing on all cylinders in a strictly social sense.

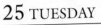

25 TUESDAY
Moon Age Day 25   Moon Sign Leo

Moneymaking concerns are one direction in which your mind is turning and you have a knowing knack of hanging on to cash you already possess. Don't be too surprised if you discover that you have an admirer you didn't suspect previously. In every sense your popularity is going off the scale.

26 WEDNESDAY
Moon Age Day 26   Moon Sign Virgo

You may meet someone today who challenges your views or who really makes you work hard to explain yourself. This is not necessarily a bad thing, especially if it shakes you out of some sort of lethargy that has overtaken you. There is little around to threaten your overall success at the moment.

27 THURSDAY
Moon Age Day 27   Moon Sign Virgo

Your desire for information is great and you spend a lot of time today casting around to make yourself even more knowledgeable. Not only do you want to know things but you also want to communicate what you have learned to others. There are gains to be made financially but not by gambling.

28 FRIDAY
Moon Age Day 28   Moon Sign Libra

Your present fondness for debate may now be put to the test and you will have to work hard to win in debates of any sort. Not that this fact troubles you because this is a period during which you are thrilled by sharpening your intellect and by getting to grips with issues that have been murky in the past.

29 SATURDAY
Moon Age Day 29   Moon Sign Libra

The drive to achieve things is getting stronger all the time but a little caution is advisable for the moment. You can be too impetuous for your own good and will be inclined to fly off the handle if things don't go the way you want them to. Exercise a little patience and count to ten before reacting.

30 SUNDAY
Moon Age Day 0   Moon Sign Libra

If ever there was a good time to start new projects, that is what this Sunday represents. You will have the time to think things through and to plan but not for long because you show a burning desire to get on and achieve something. Neither will your efforts be restricted to domestic or home-based issues.

31 MONDAY
Moon Age Day 1   Moon Sign Scorpio

If you have a pet project, now is the best time of all to work on it. Almost everyone seems to want to lend a hand and if there is any problem at all about today it lies in the fact that your very popularity makes it difficult to concentrate. Stay away from arguments that have nothing to do with you.

November 2016

1 TUESDAY
Moon Age Day 2   Moon Sign Scorpio

You are now in a position to realise some untapped potential within yourself and to use it to your advantage. In order to get the very most from the lunar high this time around you will have to be a little selfish. Don't worry too much about this because it is a very temporary matter and in most situations you remain considerate.

2 WEDNESDAY
Moon Age Day 3   Moon Sign Sagittarius

There are likely to be people around now who broaden your horizons and who furnish you with what you need to chase new ideas. You are likely to be very diplomatic at present and should get on well, even with those who can sometimes be rather awkward; but are you making all the concessions?

3 THURSDAY
Moon Age Day 4   Moon Sign Sagittarius

The more you can look towards the future, the greater is the incentive you feel at the moment. There won't be much time for living in the past and so the nostalgic side of Scorpio seems to be taking a bit of a holiday. You could find yourself getting very close to the end of something that has taken ages to complete.

4 FRIDAY
Moon Age Day 5   Moon Sign Sagittarius

You may be able to make some constructive changes today, brought about because your organisational skills are so good. At the same time you are getting the very most from personal and romantic attachments and will be doing all you can to interest and please those with whom you live.

5 SATURDAY
Moon Age Day 6   Moon Sign Capricorn

You could be some sort of pioneer today because trends show you to have a desire for adventure, in addition to a deep curiosity. Although the winter is starting to set in some Scorpio people will be choosing this time to take a holiday. If you are one of them you could have chosen wisely.

6 SUNDAY
Moon Age Day 7   Moon Sign Capricorn

Though practical aims seem to be on target, you show some impatience with limitations you cannot control. Try to stay calm, even when you think you are being provoked and fall back on your natural ability to meditate. If you are settled in yourself, most matters should work out well for you.

7 MONDAY
Moon Age Day 8   Moon Sign Aquarius

There are extended and powerful opportunities coming along now and they could have a very profound part to play in the way your life runs. New incentives at work can mean better financial prospects in the not too distant future and you may also be in line for some sort of unexpected advancement.

8 TUESDAY
Moon Age Day 9   Moon Sign Aquarius

Look for inspiration at the moment in everything you do. Life has a habit of throwing up significant object lessons and if you want to make the most of every situation you should not avoid these. A part of your mind is looking back towards what now seems to have been a truly halcyon past. A dose of realism is called for!

9 WEDNESDAY
Moon Age Day 10   Moon Sign Pisces

New friendship interests bring out the best in you. Although most of your pals have been around in your life for quite some time, an important new contact may come along now. Someone new can also bring a different way of looking at old issues, not to mention a greater realisation of your own potential.

10 THURSDAY
Moon Age Day 11   Moon Sign Pisces

You continue to show a very sensible face to the world at large and new trends also indicate how funny you can be. It ought to be very easy to keep others entertained whilst you are in this frame of mind and the world could hardly fail to notice your presence. Step up the heat in romantic attachments.

11 FRIDAY
Moon Age Day 12   Moon Sign Pisces

You are in the middle of what looks like being a rather fortunate phase in many ways. A lot of this has to do with your own attitude because you remain flexible, adaptable and fairly easily pleased. Of course you won't get on well with everyone and have a particular dislike at present for those who are selfish.

12 SATURDAY
Moon Age Day 13   Moon Sign Aries

The weekend is likely to be steady rather than overly busy and there should be time for you to work things out in your mind. There is nothing to indicate that you are withdrawing into yourself as much as might sometimes be the case but you do relish the prospect of hours spent alone, or with just one important person.

13 SUNDAY
Moon Age Day 14   Moon Sign Aries

Your ability to get important people on your side is particularly well-starred today. Your powers of persuasion have rarely been better and you are able to manipulate situations without having to try too hard. Family members could prove to be slightly intransigent but the best way to deal with this situation is to ignore it.

14 MONDAY
Moon Age Day 15   Moon Sign Taurus

This is a red light period – in other words a time when many things seem to come to a definite halt. If your expectations are not high, there is no problem. The only real difficulty is encountered when you try to push forward regardless of the consequences and without looking carefully at the implications of your actions.

15 TUESDAY
Moon Age Day 16   Moon Sign Taurus

The lunar low remains with you for today and probably slows things down considerably at the start of this working week. It is likely that you will have to rely heavily on the good offices of others, a fact that could annoy you somewhat. Don't get too bogged down with pointless details.

16 WEDNESDAY
Moon Age Day 17   Moon Sign Gemini

You lap up attention today and will take great delight in being the centre of people's consideration. This is likely to be especially true at work where your motivational skills are also good. In a more personal sense you may fail to persuade your partner that you really do know what you are talking about.

17 THURSDAY
Moon Age Day 18   Moon Sign Gemini

You might quite rightly have doubts about those who are talking big but actually producing very little. You on the other hand will not make promises you cannot follow up on and tend to be extremely reliable. Get in touch with those you know have the answers you presently need.

18 FRIDAY
Moon Age Day 19   Moon Sign Cancer

The ability to deal with practical matters in the way you did yesterday now seems to be slightly lacking. This may be as much down to the reaction of others as it is to your own nature. If there is something about which you are uncertain you could do far worse than asking someone more experienced.

19 SATURDAY
Moon Age Day 20   Moon Sign Cancer

Today you show yourself to be very resourceful and more than able to get what you want, even from potentially difficult situations. You won't take no for an answer and can be more persuasive than even Scorpio usually manages to be. Pointless rules and regulations simply make you more determined.

20 SUNDAY
Moon Age Day 21   Moon Sign Leo

Do others presently have your best interests at heart? It might appear so but you need to be slightly careful because it is entirely possible that at least one person is trying to deceive you in some way. It would be sensible to check and double-check all details today and to analyse situations very carefully.

21 MONDAY
Moon Age Day 22   Moon Sign Leo

You show yourself to be both magnetic and dynamic today and as a result it seems that others love to be around you. Put your creative powers to the test and start something new around your home. If your ideas are particularly grandiose you will want to enlist the support of other family members.

22 TUESDAY
Moon Age Day 23   Moon Sign Virgo

An issue to do with your love life may seem slightly less than inspiring today. Maybe your partner is simply not receptive to your ideas or it could be that they are simply out of sorts with themselves. Whatever the problem, you have the patience and the sensitivity to deal with it.

23 WEDNESDAY
Moon Age Day 24   Moon Sign Virgo

You look towards monetary security today and might be sitting on your purse or wallet rather than handing over cash when you don't have to do so. When dealing with younger family members you show that you are capable of being strict but fair, although you also need to explain yourself.

24 THURSDAY
Moon Age Day 25   Moon Sign Libra

Everyday affairs run smoothly enough, and you may get the chance to show just how funny you can be. Humour is the way to get what you want at the moment and this fact is hardly likely to be lost on you. All cultural interests captivate you now and your intellect is as honed as a razor.

25 FRIDAY
Moon Age Day 26   Moon Sign Libra

You may desire greater freedom but the big question is how to get it? Don't be too quick to show your independence but rather rely on the good offices and ideas of others. At work you are quick to take on responsibility and speedy in getting things done. Meanwhile, domestic matters are likely to be put on hold.

26 SATURDAY
Moon Age Day 27   Moon Sign Libra

In a social sense you are anxious to get some change working in your life. This is a very restless time for Scorpio and you won't always feel entirely comfortable with your lot. There are exciting times ahead and you instinctively realise that this is the case, even if getting things moving takes a while.

27 SUNDAY
Moon Age Day 28   Moon Sign Scorpio

This is the best time during November for taking calculated risks of any sort, though you would be well advised that throwing caution to the wind completely is not to be advised. It is clear that you know what you want, especially in your professional life, and you now have a greater chance of achieving than over the last few weeks.

28 MONDAY
Moon Age Day 29   Moon Sign Scorpio

The tide of fortune seems to be flowing your way, so much so that you are far more willing to take a chance than might usually be the case. They say that fortune favours the bold and if this is the case you are likely to get on very well today. Be brave enough to tell someone how special they are to you.

29 TUESDAY
Moon Age Day 0   Moon Sign Sagittarius

You are very inclined to take up intellectual pursuits today, whether or not they are of practical use to you. A crossword puzzle or quiz of some sort could really capture your imagination, so much so that everything else is ignored. Once again you show yourself to be single-minded.

30 WEDNESDAY *Moon Age Day 1 Moon Sign Sagittarius*

You now have the ability to go well beyond the status quo and that means really allowing your originality to shine out. The only slight drawback is that you can be a little shy when you have to stand up in front of a crowd. This is less of a problem whilst the Sun retains its present position.

December 2016

1 THURSDAY
Moon Age Day 2   Moon Sign Sagittarius

What probably matters more than anything as far as December is concerned is keeping up an active and interesting social life. That shouldn't be too difficult at this time of year but for the moment there are practicalities to be dealt with too. Help a friend to find a solution to a long-standing problem.

2 FRIDAY
Moon Age Day 3   Moon Sign Capricorn

Career prospects have much going for them at the moment and you may find that you are taking on new responsibilities or else consolidating business gains you made earlier. At the same time there are clearly going to be domestic issues that need your attention. All in all this is likely to be a very busy day.

3 SATURDAY
Moon Age Day 4   Moon Sign Capricorn

Your enthusiasm knows no bounds and from a physical point of view you are now likely to be on top form. There is probably plenty to be done at home and family members will be pleased to have you around. Maybe this is as good a time as any to get out those boxes of decorations.

4 SUNDAY
Moon Age Day 5   Moon Sign Aquarius

For those Scorpios who have recently been through slightly difficult times in a personal sense, attachments should now be easier to cope with. It may be that you can come to a new understanding or simply that your partner is now being far more reasonable. Put minor family worries to the back of your mind.

5 MONDAY
Moon Age Day 6   Moon Sign Aquarius

You continue to show a generally positive face to the world and will be quite happy to take on more work, especially when you realise that extra effort now will mean more time to yourself later. When it comes to signing documents or taking on some new financial responsibility, make sure you have read the small print.

6 TUESDAY
Moon Age Day 7   Moon Sign Aquarius

Avoid being over aggressive regarding issues that would be best dealt with in a more diplomatic way. The trouble seems to be that you know very well how situations should be handled but those around you have different ideas. You could be especially inquisitive today – maybe about a surprise gift.

7 WEDNESDAY
Moon Age Day 8   Moon Sign Pisces

Some of the gains that come along today are likely to be surprising in nature so it would be sensible to get yourself fully prepared. You could be coming to the end of a task that seems to have lasted for ages but it won't be long before you find yourself something new to act as a beacon for the future.

8 THURSDAY
Moon Age Day 9   Moon Sign Pisces

Don't be afraid to step into the limelight at some stage today. You need the accolades that are coming your way in order to boost your confidence and to make you feel special. Something you did for someone else in the past is now coming back at you in a very positive and surprising way.

9 FRIDAY
Moon Age Day 10   Moon Sign Aries

Keep up the generally fast pace and make sure that you deal with issues as and when they arise. There isn't going to be much time for practical matters later in the month and if you put in that extra bit of effort now this won't lead to problems then. All the same, do try to get a little fresh air at some stage during the day.

10 SATURDAY
Moon Age Day 11   Moon Sign Aries

This is not what could be called a good period for taking undue risks. Before the end of the day the Moon will have entered Taurus, its least favourable position as far as you are concerned. Use a little circumspection and don't be afraid to seek out some inspiration and experience when it matters the most.

11 SUNDAY
Moon Age Day 12   Moon Sign Taurus

It is your diplomatic skills that turn out to be of particular importance now. When others fall out with each other you find ways to play the honest broker. This is one of the most important gifts of Scorpio at present and it allows you to get on well with everyone. As far as your own life is concerned you should be quite cheerful.

12 MONDAY
Moon Age Day 13   Moon Sign Taurus

You may well feel the urge to break out of mundane routines this week but today is not the time to start. Approach the coming week with some caution and don't take on so much today that you get weary just thinking about it. By tomorrow the lunar low is out of the way and then it's onward and upward.

13 TUESDAY
Moon Age Day 14   Moon Sign Gemini

Getting some peace and privacy may not be easy at the moment, mostly because others are calling on your assistance all the time. If it isn't family members who demand your attention it is likely to be friends. You are unlikely to react negatively, however, because basically you need to be needed.

14 WEDNESDAY
Moon Age Day 15   Moon Sign Gemini

You are now in a position to gain greater control of your personal finances, as well as being able to impose a degree of discipline regarding the spending of younger family members. This is some achievement so close to Christmas but you have masses of good ideas for saving money.

15 THURSDAY   *Moon Age Day 16   Moon Sign Cancer*

This would be a very good time to develop your personal resources and to look towards home-based matters in greater detail. You may be more inclined to stay at home than was the case yesterday but there is plenty to keep you occupied and it is very unlikely you will be bored.

16 FRIDAY   *Moon Age Day 17   Moon Sign Cancer*

Your initiative and thinking power remain good and you know exactly what you want from any given situation, even if others flounder somewhat. You can't expect everyone to keep up with your quick thinking and there are certainly going to be times now when you will have to go it alone.

17 SATURDAY   *Moon Age Day 18   Moon Sign Leo*

This is a day during which you should avoid getting on the wrong side of others. The fact is that not everyone is equally easy to either read or to approach. If friends especially seem particularly grumpy this might be a good day to leave them alone. You can approach them better by early next week.

18 SUNDAY   *Moon Age Day 19   Moon Sign Leo*

You cannot afford to remain quiet or to lock yourself away this Sunday. You need to be out and about, enjoying what life has to offer and also learning more that will be to your own advantage eventually. Rules and regulations can get on your nerves once again, especially if they threaten to hamper your social life.

19 MONDAY   *Moon Age Day 20   Moon Sign Virgo*

Practical affairs have a great deal going for them now and in terms of money you are likely to be doing better than ever. Look for genuine bargains as far as those last minute purchases are concerned, even if that means waiting until even closer to Christmas to get what you are looking for.

20 TUESDAY ☿ *Moon Age Day 21 Moon Sign Virgo*

In your professional and work life you need to be ready to explore new ground, even though Christmas is just around the corner. You can make gains whilst others have taken their eye off the ball and this is going to be important in the New Year. In a romantic sense you tend to act on impulse now.

21 WEDNESDAY ☿ *Moon Age Day 22 Moon Sign Virgo*

This is a very favourable time for investigations of almost any sort. It seems as though you have your detective head on again and almost anything mysterious will really captivate your attention. Don't be too quick to judge others, especially regarding issues you are not entirely sure about yourself.

22 THURSDAY ☿ *Moon Age Day 23 Moon Sign Libra*

Financial opportunities and your fiscal sense remain good and you may find that you are now in a position to command a better salary – or maybe it is just that you are working longer hours and therefore earning more. Personal incentives are also good and this would be an ideal day to approach a prospective romantic partner.

23 FRIDAY ☿ *Moon Age Day 24 Moon Sign Libra*

Now your intellectual abilities and your powers of communication are reaching a peak. It would take a very cunning person to fool you in any way and the fact is that you see through situations as if they were made of glass. New creative pursuits could be on your mind and these may slightly overtake you.

24 SATURDAY ☿ *Moon Age Day 25 Moon Sign Scorpio*

Christmas Eve should find you more organised than you expected and possibly with time on your hands to do whatever takes your fancy. There is just a slight possibility that your sense of responsibility will clash with your need to find personal space but if you meditate a little you can find ways round this trend.

25 SUNDAY ☿ *Moon Age Day 26   Moon Sign Scorpio*

The green light is on for Christmas Day and action becomes possible. Don't wait to be asked today because it is very important for you to take the initiative. You respond well to the invitations that are coming in from other people and can easily handle about half a dozen different jobs at the same time.

26 MONDAY ☿ *Moon Age Day 27   Moon Sign Scorpio*

With plenty of optimism and a self-belief that is far stronger than Scorpio usually expects, you seem to be really motoring towards your objectives. Forward progress may only be slowed by the realisation that the holidays are all around you and some of your resources will have to be directed towards the celebrations.

27 TUESDAY ☿ *Moon Age Day 28   Moon Sign Sagittarius*

This ought to be another fairly good day and one during which you are still keen to travel and maybe to visit people you don't see too often throughout the year. It is possible that personal attachments will be on your mind again but now it is because love and romance seem to be offering so much.

28 WEDNESDAY ☿ *Moon Age Day 29   Moon Sign Sagittarius*

There are likely to be differences of opinion arising today, maybe over what you want to do in a social sense. You need to compromise and will have a better time if you are willing to do so. It might be good to travel a short way in order to see someone who lives at a distance or who is rarely at home.

29 THURSDAY ☿ *Moon Age Day 0   Moon Sign Capricorn*

Conflicts can arise if you sense that certain people are showing a lack of sensitivity to your own circumstances. Neither will you stand idly by if you think that a friend is being misused in any way. Scorpio's social conscience is extremely heightened under present trends and it really shows.

30 FRIDAY ☿ *Moon Age Day 1   Moon Sign Capricorn*

This is likely to be a busy period but also a deeply inspirational time. Whether or not you are at work, there is plenty to keep you occupied and no lack of incentive when it comes to showing yourself off in social situations. It appears that everyone wants be your friend.

31 SATURDAY ☿ *Moon Age Day 2   Moon Sign Capricorn*

The last day of the year will bring some pleasant surprises and maybe a social invitation that turns out to be very special. Intellectual matters stimulate your mind and you are clearly in a good mood to solve puzzles of one sort or another. The energy to see the year out with a bang is certainly not lacking.

SCORPIO:
2017 DIARY PAGES

SCORPIO:
YOUR YEAR IN BRIEF

At the very start of the year you find yourself filled with enthusiasm and longing to get on with things after an enforced break. January and February should be good, productive months. You may come across people you don't see too often and also have some very good ideas about how to get things moving in the direction you wish. Unfortunately, not everyone around you will be equally helpful.

With the arrival of the spring, March and April bring a feeling of relief because you are able to sort out an issue that has been on your mind for quite a while. Don't get stuck in negative ways of thinking as far as your home life is concerned. Discuss things with those who are close to you and come to conclusions that can suit everyone. Better financial prospects are indicated in April and some speculation is likely to take place.

May and June should find you riding high on the crest of a wave. There are professional gains to be made and you seem to have what it takes to mix business and pleasure very successfully. This is definitely a time to ask for what you want because the very worst that could happen is that someone might say no. Look after your own interests.

High summer is extremely positive and you can enjoy everything that is happening around you but without some of the minor anxieties that often attend the Scorpio life and attitude. With everything to play for in a practical sense during July and August you should be increasing your finances and in the mood to win, no matter what you set out to do. Pleasant and considerate, you nevertheless develop a competitive edge. People will really want to know you and make a beeline for your door.

If you had expected September and October to be a time when you could slow down somewhat, you will be disappointed. You will be filled with energy, determined to keep moving forward and getting other people on your side. From a professional point of view you can really shine and improved financial prospects should show themselves throughout both months. Make the most of some very favourable trends if you can.

The final months of the year, November and December, might bring apparent reversals but most of these will be followed by a realisation that things are, after all, going very much your way. You respond well to pressure, most of which is positive and you may be in for a promotion of some sort. The Christmas period should turn out to be quite enlightening as well as joyful. You are likely to finish the year on a generally positive note and with the realisation that much of what you wanted to achieve has been accomplished.

January
2017

1 SUNDAY
☿   *Moon Age Day 4*   *Moon Sign Aquarius*

The new year begins with some good social highlights, though you might find yourself somewhat distracted by the general requirements of a busy practical life too. Your thoughtful side also puts in an appearance so make sure you keep busy to avoid dark thoughts. Confidence isn't lacking, but it is of a peculiar sort.

2 MONDAY
☿   *Moon Age Day 5*   *Moon Sign Aquarius*

The pace of your everyday life increases, offering all sorts of new incentives but also leading to a need to plan carefully. It is most important to avoid exhausting yourself because if that happens, you will achieve very little. Family members may take on a special importance for a number of reasons now.

3 TUESDAY
☿   *Moon Age Day 6*   *Moon Sign Pisces*

Money-making endeavours are well highlighted today and you should discover that you have the knack of getting things right at this stage of the week. Some luck is on your side and you can continue the working week with a flourish. Look out for new incentives as far as sporting or competitive activities are concerned.

4 WEDNESDAY
☿   *Moon Age Day 7*   *Moon Sign Pisces*

Others might not view discussions and negotiations about what you see as vital issues in quite the same way. You will need to remain patient and should not allow the more brooding side of your Scorpio nature to get in the way of objectivity. It's simply that people lead busy lives and sometimes don't think enough.

5 THURSDAY ☿ *Moon Age Day 8   Moon Sign Aries*

Your power to attract the better things in life certainly seems to be improving now. You can expect a busy Thursday, but one that works mainly in your direction. If there appears to be nothing ahead but work and worry, you really are not looking at the positive side of life as much as you should so take a step back and appreciate all that life offers.

6 FRIDAY ☿ *Moon Age Day 9   Moon Sign Aries*

The acquisition of money will seem to be of special interest today. Maybe that is because your earning power is growing exponentially or because you are thinking about taking on a new and more rewarding responsibility? Whatever the reason, you will be looking over your personal finances.

7 SATURDAY ☿ *Moon Age Day 10   Moon Sign Taurus*

The Moon has entered your opposite zodiac sign of Taurus bringing the monthly lunar low, and although you are not giving in to it, it is likely to sap your energy at least a little. Settle for a stay-at-home sort of weekend and don't be too keen to push yourself too hard. This isn't the time of year during which you will want to be doing too much in any case.

8 SUNDAY *Moon Age Day 11   Moon Sign Taurus*

The lull remains in place and there doesn't seem to be a great deal you can do about it. Settle for quiet pursuits and spend time with family members. As long as you are not champing at the bit to get on with jobs that simply can't be done, there is no reason to view this as a particularly unlucky or difficult day.

9 MONDAY *Moon Age Day 12   Moon Sign Gemini*

The ups and downs of the Scorpio nature are surfacing more today than seems to have been the case for a week or two. Others might think you are moody, whereas you would merely describe yourself as pensive. Either way you will need to make that extra effort in order to show that you are ready to talk freely.

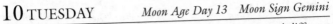

10 TUESDAY   *Moon Age Day 13   Moon Sign Gemini*

This could be a period during which you will have several different projects on the go at the same time. Avoid any tendency to rush and, if necessary, leave some of the routine tasks until later. The most important thing for today is to make sure that whatever you do, you do to the very best of your ability.

11 WEDNESDAY   *Moon Age Day 14   Moon Sign Cancer*

You could now be entering a very nostalgic period and you can this down to present astrological trends. There's no harm in looking back, unless you are searching for some magical world that never really existed. Keep at least one eye on the present and have some plans organised for the future.

12 THURSDAY   *Moon Age Day 15   Moon Sign Cancer*

Today should be quite enjoyable and offers some social highlights, a few of which you probably did not foresee. You can't expect to get everything done that you would wish and might decide to delay a few routines until a later time. If not, enlist the support of some co-operative friends.

13 FRIDAY   *Moon Age Day 16   Moon Sign Cancer*

You may feel like pushing forward today, particularly in terms of communication. It isn't hard to believe that others are listening to you more now, or that they have your best interests at heart. Although you won't be too keen to commit yourself to financial speculation at present, you could at least take a look at a potential opportunity.

14 SATURDAY   *Moon Age Day 17   Moon Sign Leo*

Whilst there is nothing at all to be gained today from sitting on the fence, that's simply the way you are feeling. This is strange for Scorpio, which usually has an opinion about everything. Perhaps you are simply being especially fair right now because you see everyone's point of view.

15 SUNDAY
Moon Age Day 18   Moon Sign Leo

Friendship and group encounters have a good feel today and you are now more willing to co-operate with others than you sometimes are. Good friends you haven't seen for some time make a return visit to your life and even general gossip is of specific interest to you right now. Plan a journey today, even if it won't take place for months.

16 MONDAY
Moon Age Day 19   Moon Sign Virgo

Certain issues at work might seem to be more trouble than they are worth now. That means leaving them alone and certainly does not indicate a period during which you should blow them up out of all proportion. With plenty to play for in the relationship stakes, don't be too embarrassed to tell people how you feel.

17 TUESDAY
Moon Age Day 20   Moon Sign Virgo

Today you should be able to impress others in most areas of your life. Attitudes vary in your friendship circle and it will become clear at some point that you cannot back everyone's point of view. Neither can you rely on diplomacy. The time has come to answer truthfully any question you are asked.

18 WEDNESDAY
Moon Age Day 21   Moon Sign Libra

The message today is to get busy and to stay that way for most of the day. If it isn't possible, you should at least make some attempt to look as though you are doing something important. This is especially true at work, where superiors are taking a great interest in your capacity to get things done and demonstrating a positive attitude will go a long way.

19 THURSDAY
Moon Age Day 22   Moon Sign Libra

There are practical situations around at the moment and you will want to take full advantage of them. You can get things done at home and seem to have a particularly good ability to organise and arrange things. All in all, this will turn out to be a busy day, but one during which you find yourself working to your full potential.

20 FRIDAY
Moon Age Day 23   Moon Sign Scorpio

This is probably the best day of the month to steam ahead at full speed. The lunar high offers all sorts of incentives, not least of all a silver tongue and the ability to lift the veil, ever so slightly, on that mysterious nature of yours. There's no doubt about the fact that you appear to be particularly attractive now.

21 SATURDAY
Moon Age Day 24   Moon Sign Scorpio

This is an excellent time to put in that extra bit of effort. New ventures should be working well and you should find yourself more than able to keep up a hectic and exciting social life. Any form of sport might seem especially attractive right now, though you will still find the time to show loved ones how much you care about them.

22 SUNDAY
Moon Age Day 25   Moon Sign Scorpio

The Sun has entered your solar fourth house bringing a new trend that should be wonderful for all matters related to your home and family. Now it is easier to get on with people who have proved difficult in the recent past and you should also find intimate relationships to be less strained than of late.

23 MONDAY
Moon Age Day 26   Moon Sign Sagittarius

Compromises are difficult to make today, especially with people at work. The fact is that you know what you want and if those around you get in the way, the responsibility is likely to be theirs. Scorpio can be quite vindictive and even a little destructive on occasions. Make sure you are not that way now.

24 TUESDAY
Moon Age Day 27   Moon Sign Sagittarius

You are more determined than ever now to get your own way. That doesn't mean you are forgetting about the needs of others. On the contrary, for every success you make, there are plenty of other people benefiting too. General good luck is on your side and you need to give her all the help you can.

25 WEDNESDAY *Moon Age Day 28   Moon Sign Capricorn*

Today marks a good period for personal matters and communications. You have the odd trick or two up your sleeve and know how to get ahead of the pack. This is an excellent time for all sporting activities, or for deciding to take a last-minute, spontaneous journey. Your confidence holds you in good stead.

26 THURSDAY *Moon Age Day 29   Moon Sign Capricorn*

Although you are very busy at the moment, this fact should not prevent you from taking on even more commitments. You tend to be in the mood to count your blessings and that means you remain generally cheerful, even on the odd occasion when things go wrong. Your patience over a particular issue will be rewarded soon.

27 FRIDAY *Moon Age Day 0   Moon Sign Capricorn*

There ought to be plenty of time for fun and games, some of a deeply personal nature. A winter holiday would suit you down to the ground at this time but if you can't get one, you could at least spend a day away from everyday routines. Thinking in terms of some impromptu shopping could please you.

28 SATURDAY *Moon Age Day 1   Moon Sign Aquarius*

This may be the very best time of the month for entertaining at home, which could be beneficial to you in more than one way. Not only will be you have the fun of preparing a slap up meal for someone, at the same time you could please a business or social contact. Clubs and societies might play a part in your thinking, too.

29 SUNDAY *Moon Age Day 2   Moon Sign Aquarius*

At the moment, making progress means being in the know. That is why you have to keep your eyes and ears open. The more you pay attention to what is happening around you, the greater is your chance of keeping up. This is particularly true for Scorpios who work at the weekend or who hold significant professional responsibility.

30 MONDAY   *Moon Age Day 3   Moon Sign Pisces*

The current pace of activity shows no sign at all of slowing. Remember that you are only human and, if necessary, force yourself into a way of living that allows time for rest and reflection. It might be possible to look at your routines and itemise those jobs that could wait until later.

31 TUESDAY   *Moon Age Day 4   Moon Sign Pisces*

There is a slight possibility that some strong disagreements might crop up today. Such a state of affairs will only happen if those around you insist on being right all the time. For your own part, the present planetary line-up can make you stubborn and unwilling to admit that you could just be wrong about something.

February 2017

1 WEDNESDAY
Moon Age Day 5   Moon Sign Aries

This is a day during which you probably will not have to struggle too much materially. Worldly goods more or less automatically come your way as and when you need them. Some of this could come about as a result of the assistance on offer from others. Make the most of this, plus your tendency to be particularly affectionate at this time.

2 THURSDAY
Moon Age Day 6   Moon Sign Aries

You continue to gain a great deal from friendly assistance right now and from being willing to do what others ask of you. This is a social day and one that proves how much you are loved and respected by others. Even though you are extremely friendly and generally interested it might be hard to do more than one thing at a time.

3 FRIDAY
Moon Age Day 7   Moon Sign Aries

An emotional issue may demand your attention today. Spend some time dealing with that but don't allow it to divert you from social and enjoyable situations. Although you may no longer be getting everything you want in a material sense today, there are greater gains on the way.

4 SATURDAY
Moon Age Day 8   Moon Sign Taurus

If it feels that the world is against you, all you have to realise is that you are not being exactly positive yourself, thanks to the lunar low. Patience is important, together with a willingness to stand back and watch for a while. Don't assume that you will be able to do many different things at the same time today – you won't.

5 SUNDAY
Moon Age Day 9   Moon Sign Taurus

Your spirits and enthusiasm could be rather low again today. Once again, you have to understand that this short trend can be used in a positive way. Trying to overturn obstacles now merely means wasting energy. Instead, watch and wait. By tomorrow the Moon will have moved on and you should be entirely back on form.

6 MONDAY
Moon Age Day 10   Moon Sign Gemini

You may be filled with ingenious ideas, and yet lack the ability to put some of them into practice. Seek out people who are in the know and look particularly for specialist help. In terms of relationships you will now be discovering individuals who have a greater fondness for you than you previously realised.

7 TUESDAY
Moon Age Day 11   Moon Sign Gemini

Socially speaking this is a day that is potentially filled with joy. With plenty of energy again and a real need to paint the town red look out for people who have a good idea how to have fun too. Any real problems associated with work ought to be disappearing quite rapidly, leaving you feeling generally contented with your life.

8 WEDNESDAY
Moon Age Day 12   Moon Sign Cancer

The most fulfilling moments you will experience at this time come from home and private matters. These tend to drive you back down inside yourself, which is not always a bad thing for sensitive Scorpio. Everyday routines should be easy to deal with and some of them might actually be welcomed at this time.

9 THURSDAY
Moon Age Day 13   Moon Sign Cancer

Though you should avoid being side-tracked by trivia of any sort, that doesn't mean you should also stay away from enjoyment and entertainment. You need balance in your life at present and committing yourself to nothing but work is hardly likely to be fulfilling. Spend some time in the company of loved ones if you can.

10 FRIDAY
Moon Age Day 14   Moon Sign Leo

A change of plan in terms of family arrangements could turn out to be a good thing as the weekend approaches. You have to respond to altering values and ideas – not merely your own but those of others too. Your confidence isn't lacking, though you will need to qualify a few of your thoughts right now.

11 SATURDAY
Moon Age Day 15   Moon Sign Leo

You are probably out of the professional mainstream for the weekend and that's just as well. Social possibilities are far more important to you at this time and mixing with interesting friends and acquaintances gets your mind working in new ways. This is hardly likely to be a conventional day, but it could be one you will enjoy.

12 SUNDAY
Moon Age Day 16   Moon Sign Virgo

You could be stopped in your tracks by a personal matter, possibly one arising at home. As long as you are prepared to discuss matters honestly, this won't prove awkward or get in your way too much. It is vitally important at this stage of the month that those around you know how you genuinely feel.

13 MONDAY
Moon Age Day 17   Moon Sign Virgo

It could be that professional matters are going less smoothly than you would wish. It will be important to back your hunches and your instinct will be not to waste time saying when you could be doing. However, take care not to rush into things and set aside some time to spend with people you really like.

14 TUESDAY
Moon Age Day 18   Moon Sign Libra

Your ideas and opinions are subject to criticism today. Since this is part of a planetary process that leads towards advancement it is important that you see things in this light. Try not to get annoyed because you are being asked questions that seem to test your resolve – you will find the answers.

15 WEDNESDAY   *Moon Age Day 19   Moon Sign Libra*

This might be a good time for a change of scene. Get away from the everyday routines and find some way to enjoy yourself, if only for a few hours. All work and no play makes anyone dull, and particularly Scorpio today. Vitality and enthusiasm are always greater when you are genuinely interested in life and your surroundings.

16 THURSDAY   *Moon Age Day 20   Moon Sign Libra*

You should be getting the most from pleasure and leisure pursuits and may be in the mood for some luxury. Scorpions are sometimes happy to spoil themselves terribly and today is such a time. Just remember that there are practical jobs to be done first and that time should not be wasted at the moment.

17 FRIDAY   *Moon Age Day 21   Moon Sign Scorpio*

The Moon moves into your zodiac sign, bringing with it a greater determination and masses of popularity. Conversations of any sort can bring you more of what you want, whilst general good luck tends to follow you around. Now is the time to take those hunches and to back them all the way.

18 SATURDAY   *Moon Age Day 22   Moon Sign Scorpio*

Look at today as a day for getting ahead and a time when you simply have to snap your fingers in order to get your heart's desire. If you don't manage to make progress right now, you probably are not putting in quite the amount of effort necessary. Count on the support of friends, focus and throw yourself into things.

19 SUNDAY   *Moon Age Day 23   Moon Sign Sagittarius*

You are more or less filled with confidence at present and should be making short work of the sort of tasks that sometimes make you feel apprehensive. Family members are likely to be turning to you for the kind of help you are very good at offering. The slight selfish streak that is sometimes inherent in the Scorpio nature is now diminishing.

20 MONDAY
Moon Age Day 24   Moon Sign Sagittarius

When you are with close friends you should be very happy, though there is a slight chance that you lose some of the confidence you have been showing in public settings. What does remain absolutely intact is your sense of humour, which could easily see you through a potentially embarrassing situation.

21 TUESDAY
Moon Age Day 25   Moon Sign Sagittarius

On the ideas front, you might discover that you are more sluggish than you were earlier in the month. Be willing to think things through carefully and avoid any tendency to rush your decisions. That little green-eyed monster jealousy is never far from the surface with Scorpio, but don't be possessed by him as you sometimes are.

22 WEDNESDAY
Moon Age Day 26   Moon Sign Capricorn

Trends suggest that a favourable period for all domestic matters is clearly underway now. Family relationships should be close and people are likely to turn to you willingly for help and advice. Don't be too willing to spill all the beans, though. There are some things others don't want to know, no matter what they say.

23 THURSDAY
Moon Age Day 27   Moon Sign Capricorn

There are times to be quiet and other times during which you should be prepared to make a great deal of noise. Today is a noisy day and you will get far more of what you want if you are willing to tell people what you think. Few people will stand in your way because you appear so powerful.

24 FRIDAY
Moon Age Day 28   Moon Sign Aquarius

Act with determination today, particularly when you know you are being watched. It isn't the weekend yet and you will be expected to put in quite a lot of effort ahead of Saturday. By the time the working day is over you will be quite pleased to enjoy yourself during a social Friday evening, maybe in the company of good friends?

25 SATURDAY   *Moon Age Day 0   Moon Sign Aquarius*

This is a day for optimum enjoyment, which is generally easier to achieve at the weekend. If you do have to work, you can make unexpected progress. In social situations you are quite dynamic and can easily make a good impression. Someone not far away makes it plain they think you are stunning.

26 SUNDAY   *Moon Age Day 1   Moon Sign Aquarius*

You will want to be around your favourite people today, even if that means you can't do quite as you might wish. Tasks you don't wish to perform seem to be left on the back burner right now and you are probably inclined to show a rather negative face to those who try to motivate you to tackle them. It's Sunday, so a little relaxation can't be a bad thing.

27 MONDAY   *Moon Age Day 2   Moon Sign Pisces*

Keep any self-righteous behaviour under lock and key because you don't have any time for it at present. Today tends to offer a great deal of what you expect, so it's obvious what a negative attitude is likely to achieve. Stick to what you know at work but try something new when it comes to your social life.

28 TUESDAY   *Moon Age Day 3   Moon Sign Pisces*

Creative efforts go well, so much of the day could be spent doing something interesting at home. Keep your personal life to yourself for the moment and don't let too many people in on your secrets. When it comes to financial issues, you could do worse than to talk things through with your partner or a family member.

2017

1 WEDNESDAY
Moon Age Day 4   Moon Sign Aries

This is a good time to be around your favourite people. You can gain a great deal simply from being in the company of those you like, which could well extend to specific family members. Try to avoid listening to gossip at the moment. It is highly likely that you will get hold of the wrong end of the stick, which can cause all kinds of problems.

2 THURSDAY
Moon Age Day 5   Moon Sign Aries

Though in a career sense you may notice new possibilities in the offing, your love life could easily seem less than satisfying. Perhaps you are causing the problem? It is worth taking a look at your general attitude and forcing a degree of flexibility to come into your general patterns of thinking.

3 FRIDAY
Moon Age Day 6   Moon Sign Taurus

A wind-down period is at hand, thanks to the arrival of the lunar low. It won't have too much of a bearing on your life this month, unless you decide that you are going to move any mountains. Leave all important plans for another day and be quite content to sit and watch life go by for a few hours.

4 SATURDAY
Moon Age Day 7   Moon Sign Taurus

Once again, you tend to be quieter than of late and inclined to play your cards close to your chest. Confirming your strengths will have to wait because, for the moment at least, you notice your failings more than your skills. As long as you realise this is nothing more than a small hiccup, all should be well.

5 SUNDAY *Moon Age Day 8 Moon Sign Gemini*

Others may find you to be somewhat argumentative when it comes to general discussions today. It is important at this time to give certain individuals the benefit of the doubt and not to push too hard to gain your own objectives. You will get what you want from life soon enough, so don't rush into conversations you may later regret.

6 MONDAY *Moon Age Day 9 Moon Sign Gemini*

Career-wise it appears that you are in a risk-taking mood. That's fine as long as your gambles are genuinely calculated ones. It won't be easy to conform to the expectations others have of you at present and it is important to stretch yourself in some way. Plan now for what could turn out to be a fairly exciting period ahead.

7 TUESDAY *Moon Age Day 10 Moon Sign Cancer*

The Sun in its present position predicts that you are going to let your light shine brightly today. Go for excitement if you can, and for mixing with people you find to be especially stimulating. Intersperse the genuine needs of the day with periods during which you simply set out to have a good time.

8 WEDNESDAY *Moon Age Day 11 Moon Sign Cancer*

Your sense of self-importance is high enough today to cause you some concern if it isn't being echoed by the way others are behaving towards you. Being at the heart of things does come naturally at the moment and this may partly be because you are demanding that those around you sit up and notice that you are around.

9 THURSDAY *Moon Age Day 12 Moon Sign Leo*

Times change quickly and now having fun and enjoying yourself is your number one priority. You will be happy to spend time in the company of like-minded people, and young Scorpios especially will be burning the candle at both ends. Try to do something new and interesting on as many occasions today as you can.

10 FRIDAY
Moon Age Day 13   Moon Sign Leo

Trends change again and getting organised is what it's all about today. Of course you can rely on the assistance that comes from the direction of your friends but in the main you will want to do it all for yourself. Socially speaking you should be in the market for a good time but the odd few little personal difficulties could surface.

11 SATURDAY
Moon Age Day 14   Moon Sign Virgo

You might be rather too concerned with what is going on at home to make the best of some of the more practical aspects of life out in the world. Don't allow yourself to get stuck in a rut and do what you can to move matters forward efficiently. Once again you could be in the market for love and won't have far to look for it.

12 SUNDAY
Moon Age Day 15   Moon Sign Virgo

Work matters can be disappointing now if you happen to be a Scorpio who has to labour on at the weekend. For socially minded types there is plenty to keep you occupied. Staying away from things that you know are not good for you is going to be hard. In some cases it's a battle you might lose.

13 MONDAY
Moon Age Day 16   Moon Sign Virgo

A light-hearted touch goes a long way at the beginning of this week. Although you may feel that you are being asked to do more than you consider to be your responsibility, if you accept these challenges with good grace you will impress superiors and turn a few heads. You might try the odd cautious gamble now – the odder the better.

14 TUESDAY
Moon Age Day 17   Moon Sign Libra

Getting ahead practically is the name of the game right now. All those little jobs that you have been lining up turn out to be a piece of cake and your capacity for work knows no bounds. The odd, the unusual and the downright curious appeal to you greatly and stimulate that quirky Scorpio nature.

15 WEDNESDAY   *Moon Age Day 18   Moon Sign Libra*

Work and routines could be affected by minor mishaps. It helps to check and double-check situations at this time and to avoid embarking on anything too adventurous. A sense of proportion in matters of love and relationships can be particularly useful and you will find that your friends are especially helpful.

16 THURSDAY   *Moon Age Day 19   Moon Sign Scorpio*

You can look forward to situations generally turning out more or less as you would wish today. The lunar high brings better luck and an ability for you to use what comes your way more completely. You won't be too concerned about rules and regulations, many of which will get on your nerves.

17 FRIDAY   *Moon Age Day 20   Moon Sign Scorpio*

Getting a great deal done is par for the course this Friday. An ideal time for shopping, travelling, going out with friends and doing a host of other things that are right up your street. In personal relationships you value give and take and will be fun to have around under most circumstances.

18 SATURDAY   *Moon Age Day 21   Moon Sign Scorpio*

Personal co-operation with co-workers offers good results today, so it's worth making sure you know what others are doing. Away from work, some minor problems that may have arisen in the family seem to be putting themselves right. This means a happier home life and plenty of laughs.

19 SUNDAY   *Moon Age Day 22   Moon Sign Sagittarius*

You can look forward to warm responses from a host of other people, not least of all those individuals you care for deeply. Young Scorpios, or those who have been actively looking for love, should not be disappointed at present. However, you will almost certainly have to make part of the running yourself to this is not a time to be shy.

20 MONDAY
Moon Age Day 23   Moon Sign Sagittarius

There are too many strong opinions about today and if you insist on offering your own, trouble could be the result. Better by far to remain neutral and refuse to get involved. The quiet side of Scorpio could well be on display, a fact that could just come as a surprise to people who have been seeing a more gregarious you recently.

21 TUESDAY
Moon Age Day 24   Moon Sign Capricorn

Times change quickly and you are footloose and fancy-free today, and in just the right frame of mind to get what you want. You don't achieve this objective by being difficult or pushy. On the contrary, you are sweetness itself and inclined to do as many favours as there are hours in the day.

22 WEDNESDAY
Moon Age Day 25   Moon Sign Capricorn

Romantic attachments tend to be positively highlighted now. Interesting encounters are also on the cards and once again you show a particular preference for anything odd, unusual or curious. Be prepared to change direction at a moment's notice if your intuition tells you this would be the best thing to do.

23 THURSDAY
Moon Age Day 26   Moon Sign Capricorn

A new phase begins that enhances all aspects of work and practical life. The Sun is now in your solar sixth house, where it will remain for the next month or so. In hard and fast terms this helps you to get things done and also provides just the mental stimulus you need to get on with new projects.

24 FRIDAY
Moon Age Day 27   Moon Sign Aquarius

You may have to contend with some disagreeable individuals around now. Although it will be necessary to show a civil attitude to them, you certainly don't have to like the people in question. What won't help today is losing your temper. This is a time when it is necessary to count to ten – more than once if necessary.

25 SATURDAY   *Moon Age Day 28   Moon Sign Aquarius*

There is much to keep you reassured about life today, though mainly behind closed doors and when you are in the company of your partner or lover. Show the sultry and even the sexy side of your nature around this time – that is if you want to get the best response. Practical matters can be fraught with potential problems.

26 SUNDAY   *Moon Age Day 29   Moon Sign Pisces*

You can take almost any aspect of life in your stride today. Whilst this is certainly not the most interesting part of the month, there are gains to be made. How Sunday turns out depends entirely on you. Most planetary trends are neutral, allowing a good deal of leeway and plenty of scope for good times.

27 MONDAY   *Moon Age Day 0   Moon Sign Pisces*

You get by today by using your personal magnetism, which is quite high. A slightly disruptive phase in work matters doesn't really matter too much because most of your private thoughts today are dedicated to having fun in one way or another. Plan holidays now or, if you are especially lucky, take a break from the late winter weather.

28 TUESDAY   *Moon Age Day 1   Moon Sign Aries*

You can happily depend on the help and support that comes from the direction of others today. Instead of struggling with matters you are not able to resolve, turn to someone who has more experience than you do. Conversation, even at a casual level, carries instructions you simply have to follow.

29 WEDNESDAY   *Moon Age Day 2   Moon Sign Aries*

A little soul-searching may be necessary, particularly if you think you have been somewhat unfair to someone you care for deeply. It would be best to come clean and to make a full confession. Once that is out of the way, get on with enjoying yourself, especially when you are surrounded by people with a positive attitude.

30 THURSDAY
Moon Age Day 3   Moon Sign Taurus

Some tests of your patience are now on the cards. What doesn't help is that you are rather impetuous at the moment and less inclined than usual to settle for routines. Thus you could find yourself thrust into a somewhat frustrating day. The way to deal with the situation is to spend some periods of time on your own.

31 FRIDAY
Moon Age Day 4   Moon Sign Taurus

The lunar low probably means settling for second best, or at least that's the way things will look at first. As long as you are aware that this is a good time for relaxation, all should be well. Tomorrow some of the slightly negative influences disappear but for the moment try not to push yourself and opt for a little well-deserved rest instead.

April

1 SATURDAY
Moon Age Day 5   Moon Sign Gemini

Today should bring out all the interesting elements in your social life. It appears that your curiosity is roused over many different issues and that makes you interested and interesting. Friends tend to gather round you at this time and will almost certainly have some fascinating news to impart.

2 SUNDAY
Moon Age Day 6   Moon Sign Gemini

Harmonious trends now surround you, especially in the areas of love and romance. You are very approachable at this time and show the most loving side of your Scorpio nature. This also tends to make you rather protective of your partner – perhaps a little too much so in some cases. Remember they need space to breathe!

3 MONDAY
Moon Age Day 7   Moon Sign Cancer

In terms of your career you can expect minor setbacks at the moment. These are not of any real importance, though they might appear to be so at first. Don't be afraid to abandon something completely if you know it will lead to a fresh start. Although somewhat hesitant today, you really need to grasp the nettle and be dynamic.

4 TUESDAY
Moon Age Day 8   Moon Sign Cancer

Even though you are rather ingenious and forward looking in most respects there are some restrictions around at the moment. For one thing certain other parties will not allow you to have your own way, and this will really go against the grain. Try to be patient with others, but also with yourself.

5 WEDNESDAY
Moon Age Day 9   Moon Sign Leo

It should not be hard to find a warm welcome wherever you choose to go today. The midweek period strengthens your social impulses and makes it almost vital for you to mix with other people. Spending long periods on your own is not to be recommended at present, and neither is sulking when things don't go your way.

6 THURSDAY
Moon Age Day 10   Moon Sign Leo

Meetings with others could stimulate new ideas and alternative ways of looking at life. Stay away from situations that promote boredom and try to keep your life as interesting as you can. There could be one or two minor frustrations related to personal attachments and it is important not to overreact to them, but take them in your stride.

7 FRIDAY
Moon Age Day 11   Moon Sign Leo

Monetary problems may surface and you will have to do some careful thinking before you part with cash at the moment. You might also find difficulties in dealing with institutions, especially banks and insurance companies. Keep your cool and remember that the people you deal with are not the companies they represent.

8 SATURDAY
Moon Age Day 12   Moon Sign Virgo

Practical assistance may prove easy to come by today and you could do worse than allowing some sort of expert to lend you a hand. Keep away from contentious issues and try to keep life as steady and easy as possible. Although you are up for enjoyment it tends to be of a fairly subdued sort.

9 SUNDAY
Moon Age Day 13   Moon Sign Virgo

You will probably find that this is a highly social sort of Sunday, which allows you to mix freely with a host of different people. Your imagination is strong and you are likely to be thinking up new schemes to pep up your life. Quieter times may follow by the evening, when you should be pleased to put your feet up.

10 MONDAY ☿ *Moon Age Day 14 Moon Sign Libra*

You could so easily fall foul of others in discussions today. Arguing is not to be recommended. It is better by far to bite your tongue than to say something you are certain to regret later. Not everyone appears to be on your side at the moment but, in the final analysis, perhaps you should look in a mirror. The root of some of the problems may lie at your own door.

11 TUESDAY ☿ *Moon Age Day 15 Moon Sign Libra*

On an emotional level you are now calmer and better able to see situations in their true light. Getting ahead of yourself at work should be easy and that allows time later to do exactly what you want. If you don't have to commit yourself professionally at this time you will want to find ways to really enjoy yourself.

12 WEDNESDAY ☿ *Moon Age Day 16 Moon Sign Scorpio*

Make tracks as soon as possible and begin to push forward with especially favoured plans. The lunar high allows you great scope and good dexterity. Now is the period of the month when you actively can choose to put yourself to the test. Socially speaking, you should be on extremely good form.

13 THURSDAY ☿ *Moon Age Day 17 Moon Sign Scorpio*

You are filled with get-up-and-go, which is fine for you but might exhaust everyone else. This is a time when you can get on extremely well at work and a day that offers much in the way of diversion. Keep abreast of news and views. In romantic settings you shine like the sun and really can turn heads.

14 FRIDAY ☿ *Moon Age Day 18 Moon Sign Scorpio*

Avoid confusion by sorting situations out right from the start. It could be difficult for you to really understand what makes your nearest and dearest tick at present. If this turns out to be the case the most obvious course of action is to ask. Keep plugging away at a puzzle or a problem that has been on your mind.

15 SATURDAY ☿ *Moon Age Day 19*   *Moon Sign Sagittarius*

Don't make any instant decisions today. It would be far better to think matters through carefully, rather than rushing at stopgap measures. When it comes to major decisions that have a bearing on the longer-term aspects of life you could do worse than to seek the help and support of friends with some inside knowledge of the situation.

16 SUNDAY ☿ *Moon Age Day 20*   *Moon Sign Sagittarius*

You are well in charge of practical issues, though probably floundering somewhat when it comes to controlling family members who are reluctant to see sense. Don't start arguments, or even take part in them. The best way to achieve your objectives right now is to discuss matters sensibly and remain calm at all times.

17 MONDAY ☿ *Moon Age Day 21*   *Moon Sign Capricorn*

You may decide that the limelight is not at all where you want to be. Whether this turns out to be the case really depends on circumstances. If you find yourself pushed forward, particularly with regard to matters you understand well, you might find it impossible to play the shrinking violet.

18 TUESDAY ☿ *Moon Age Day 22*   *Moon Sign Capricorn*

Your love life tends to continue in a generally positive way, especially so if you are just at the start of a new personal commitment. Be willing to give ground if a potential dispute should arise at work. It won't hurt you to do so and your colleagues and superiors will respect you all the more for your reasonable attitude.

19 WEDNESDAY ☿ *Moon Age Day 23*   *Moon Sign Capricorn*

It's time to trip the light fantastic. You are filled with energy, bouncing with fun and raring to get going. If other people don't seem half as enthusiastic as you are, then it will be up to you to offer them a little nudge. If congratulations are in order regarding the life of a friend, be the first one to offer them generously.

20 THURSDAY ☿ *Moon Age Day 24   Moon Sign Aquarius*

Relationships can throw up the odd challenge and make it difficult for you to have the clear path ahead that you seem to need at the moment. Small problems come along and it's up to you to deal with them one at a time. What you should not be doing right now is biting off more than you can reasonably chew in any respect.

21 FRIDAY ☿ *Moon Age Day 25   Moon Sign Aquarius*

Your desires regarding major ambitions are getting stronger by the moment. This is a time during which you can move veritable mountains on the way to getting what you want from life. On a slightly negative note, it could be harder to win the affections of someone you feel doesn't like you much. Simply be patient.

22 SATURDAY ☿ *Moon Age Day 26   Moon Sign Pisces*

A continued emphasis on practical issues sees you taking this weekend by the scruff of the neck and positively making it do what you want. That won't suit everyone but it's impossible to do so at the moment. Money matters ought to be taking a turn for the better, with improved financial prospects showing up all the time.

23 SUNDAY ☿ *Moon Age Day 27   Moon Sign Pisces*

In terms of everyday life, this is likely to be a very busy day and without any of the relaxation that you might have reasonably expected on a Sunday. This fact is unlikely to worry you too much because you will be enjoying the cut and thrust of a full and active period.

24 MONDAY ☿ *Moon Age Day 28   Moon Sign Pisces*

Trends suggest that situations at work will move ahead more quickly now than you might have been expecting. You need to be very proactive today. Don't follow issues, but make them. People don't expect you to show the level of executive ability that is obvious in your nature right now and you can catch them off guard as a result.

25 TUESDAY ☿ *Moon Age Day 0   Moon Sign Aries*

It appears that your partner could prove to be quite demanding, though maybe without any specific control of the situation. You are well placed to offer assistance, not only to them, but also to friends who are turning to you with their own brand of problems. Scorpio is at its sensitive best today.

26 WEDNESDAY ☿ *Moon Age Day 1   Moon Sign Aries*

Emotional involvement in tricky matters can prove to be very satisfying, even though it may not start out that way as today commences. Opt for a change of scene or even a few hours at the shops. Should you need to undertake tasks that really go against the grain, you will be most displeased and likely to let your feelings be known.

27 THURSDAY ☿ *Moon Age Day 2   Moon Sign Taurus*

This is not likely to be the most favourable part of the month. The lunar low saps your reserves of energy and makes you more likely to give in rather than to push back against difficulties. You can find some confidence when you have the patience to look for it, but that might not be too often today.

28 FRIDAY ☿ *Moon Age Day 3   Moon Sign Taurus*

The lunar low is still around, though it ought to prove to be less of a problem today. For one thing your strongly social side has returned, making it easier for you to get on with people on all levels. Spend at least part of today researching something. The effort will do you good and should prove productive.

29 SATURDAY ☿ *Moon Age Day 4   Moon Sign Gemini*

Emotions are close to the surface, especially when you are dealing with people who seem to be quite unreasonable in their attitude and expectations. It would be sensible to take some time out, to simply recharge your batteries. In a social sense you should stick with people you both know and like.

30 SUNDAY ☿ *Moon Age Day 5   Moon Sign Gemini*

There is a temptation to scatter your energies more than is necessary at present. It would be better by far to concentrate on one or two really important tasks and to leave other jobs until another day. When you can't tackle something yourself, you may well find that there is someone around who can if you look hard enough.

May

2017

1 MONDAY ☿ *Moon Age Day 6   Moon Sign Cancer*

Expectations are raised in a professional sense, making you anxious to get ahead whilst opportunities present themselves. Concern for family members who seem to be having problems at present are probably not at all necessary and it would be sensible to take a second look before committing yourself to drastic action.

2 TUESDAY ☿ *Moon Age Day 7   Moon Sign Cancer*

You may have to deal with a few precarious emotional issues today. Try not to react too strongly to the fact that others are behaving in what you see as an irrational way. From their point of view it is likely that you are also acting strangely. All that is required is a little patience all round.

3 WEDNESDAY ☿ *Moon Age Day 8   Moon Sign Leo*

Matters from the past are apt to come into your mind today, forcing you down memory lane. Of course this is quite natural for Scorpio on occasions but you should try to avoid being too captivated by events from long ago. Right now it would be better to set your sights on the future and leave the past where it belongs.

4 THURSDAY *Moon Age Day 9   Moon Sign Leo*

Relationships can prove to be extremely helpful in a variety of different ways. Social encounters are especially enjoyable and ought to offer you a wealth of new ideas. From a financial perspective you will almost certainly find yourself slightly better off than you may have been expecting to be at this stage of the month.

5 FRIDAY
Moon Age Day 10   Moon Sign Virgo

Although you now feel slightly less in control of your own life than you might wish, relinquishing a little of the control would probably be no bad thing. There are people around who would be only too happy to have you rely on them; a psychological imperative that is necessary to their own wellbeing.

6 SATURDAY
Moon Age Day 11   Moon Sign Virgo

Though for today you feel the need to assert your ideas to others at home, this is less easy out there in the wider world. You might have trouble getting through to types who think about life in a very different way to you. Allowing those around you to be what they naturally are is essential, but you can't necessarily emulate them.

7 SUNDAY
Moon Age Day 12   Moon Sign Libra

There are uplifting experiences coming your way in a social sense. Although you now get on extremely well with your friends, family members could be a different kettle of fish altogether. Balancing the needs of professional, practical and personal life may not be too easy but in the end you should be able to manage well enough.

8 MONDAY
Moon Age Day 13   Moon Sign Libra

It may not be easy to put your finger on potential sources of tension at the moment. In all likelihood, they have something to do with your own restlessness. This is a time when you really could do with some travel, though mundane events are likely to prevent that from being a realistic possibility.

9 TUESDAY
Moon Age Day 14   Moon Sign Libra

Social matters should keep up your spirits today but the best times lie just around the corner. If there is anything you want to do, plan to get cracking tomorrow. For the moment, enjoy the company of people you care about and don't do more than you have to in a practical sense.

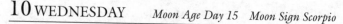

10 WEDNESDAY   *Moon Age Day 15   Moon Sign Scorpio*

The lunar high comes around again and this is clearly one of the best days of the month for getting something you really want. Persuading other people that your point of view is both valid and reasonable ought to be extremely easy and you can gain a great deal, simply from being in the right place at a time when a few words can work wonders.

11 THURSDAY   *Moon Age Day 16   Moon Sign Scorpio*

The pursuit of money may not be high on your agenda at the moment, which could be a shame because this is the time when you can attract it easily. Nevertheless this is a very positive day and a time when social impulses are extremely strong. Give yourself fully to some new sport or pastime.

12 FRIDAY   *Moon Age Day 17   Moon Sign Sagittarius*

Now you enter a time when you feel well able to express yourself. Concern for family members is less well accented now than has been the case recently and a sense of freedom begins to prevail. Most important of all you should not find it very difficult to implement some of those important changes to your life.

13 SATURDAY   *Moon Age Day 18   Moon Sign Sagittarius*

You will almost certainly find this to be an important day when it comes to busy preparations of one sort or another. Weekend working Scorpios should discover new ways to get ahead, even contemplating new forms of responsibility. Confidence remains generally high for most of today.

14 SUNDAY   *Moon Age Day 19   Moon Sign Sagittarius*

Conforming to the expectations that others have of you isn't going to be easy today. The fact is that an independent streak is greatly in evidence at this time. Your confidence remains generally high but you will have to vary your approach and even back-track on occasion. You might feel as though something is missing from your life.

15 MONDAY *Moon Age Day 20* *Moon Sign Capricorn*

At the start of the working week, along comes a boost to work and all practical matters. Now you can really concentrate on the job at hand and get through masses of tasks. It may seem a long way to an objective that you are working hard to achieve but with every hour you get closer to being where you would wish.

16 TUESDAY *Moon Age Day 21* *Moon Sign Capricorn*

Spread your efforts around a little today because you presently have a good ability to do more than one thing at a time. At the same time, you are good at registering connections between specific aspects of life. Your understanding of others is second to none at the moment.

17 WEDNESDAY *Moon Age Day 22* *Moon Sign Aquarius*

This is a day for positive social relations, as well as for coming to terms with the changing ideas and attitudes of family members. Personal contact with others is raised to an art form, whilst practical matters are now inclined to take a back seat. Be sure to tell your partner how much they mean to you.

18 THURSDAY *Moon Age Day 23* *Moon Sign Aquarius*

You will probably prefer to be on the move today because staying in one place would seem boring whilst present planetary trends are in operation. Some lucky Scorpio people will see this as an ideal time for taking an early holiday. Even if you are not one of them, you can make an enjoyable shorter journey.

19 FRIDAY *Moon Age Day 24* *Moon Sign Pisces*

This would be a wonderful time for an intimate encounter. If you are looking for love, you should certainly keep your eyes open now, and make the most of every romantic opportunity that comes along. In a more practical sense, don't turn down the chance of taking on more responsibility if there is financial promise.

20 SATURDAY
Moon Age Day 25   Moon Sign Pisces

Relationships of all kinds can keep you happy and fulfilled at the moment. Try to lead a clean life, staying away from too many junk foods and additives. Scorpio is inclined towards some very minor ill health around now, but if you are careful, you can avoid these problems altogether.

21 SUNDAY
Moon Age Day 26   Moon Sign Pisces

Your chart for today suggests that there will be a degree of restlessness to deal with. How you go about addressing this fact is up to you, but you won't help the situation by choosing to settle yourself down to a whole host of boring routines. 'Off with the old and on with the new' seems to be the best adage at the present time.

22 MONDAY
Moon Age Day 27   Moon Sign Aries

The ways in which you share feelings with those around you are under scrutiny at the start of this week. Really explaining what makes you tick is not easy but planetary influences show a greater degree of honesty on your part. You will be surprised at the results when those you care for get a better glimpse at the real you.

23 TUESDAY
Moon Age Day 28   Moon Sign Aries

Personal security needs looking at right now. This might involve money concerns, or even securing your property against thieves. The most likely explanation of all is that you are feeling a little nervous about situations that are nowhere near as difficult as they might at first appear. Don't over-react to suggestions that in reality are nothing to worry about unduly.

24 WEDNESDAY
Moon Age Day 29   Moon Sign Taurus

It might be best today to let others take some of the major decisions. With the Moon in your opposite sign of Taurus, you won't find yourself to be in a particularly spectacular frame of mind. This is not to suggest you are in for an unpleasant day, merely that you should take a back seat.

25 THURSDAY   *Moon Age Day 0   Moon Sign Taurus*

Risk-taking should be avoided and you should be very sure of your ground before you embark on any dangerous or even potentially awkward ventures. Keep life easy and steady, enjoying the company of friends and spending wisely. By tomorrow, the whole accent of your life should be looking different and life will be on the up.

26 FRIDAY   *Moon Age Day 1   Moon Sign Gemini*

There is a more decisive edge to your nature now and you will be inclined to act on impulse. Because you are feeling bolder and more able to take the initiative, the world at large falls in line. Don't be too quick to take offence at some offhand comments. They were probably not aimed at you in any case.

27 SATURDAY   *Moon Age Day 2   Moon Sign Gemini*

Your desire for freedom is definitely accentuated, as a bevy of planets cause you to look beyond the confines of your general life. A considered approach works best, though that is hardly likely to be the outcome. Before you make any rash decisions, it would be worthwhile consulting relatives, friends or your partner.

28 SUNDAY   *Moon Age Day 3   Moon Sign Cancer*

Being right is of special importance to you today, maybe because you are dealing with important issues that you sense have a big part to play in your life henceforth. Don't be put off by people who don't seem to have a great deal of confidence in you. They will come round in the end, if you simply keep plugging away solidly.

29 MONDAY   *Moon Age Day 4   Moon Sign Cancer*

Now is the time to really take stock of where you are going, and how you intend to get there. Most likely, you are thinking about your working life. Some Scorpions may take the opportunity this year to change their jobs altogether. Maybe you will be one of them, but a great deal of thought is necessary first. Always look before you leap.

30 TUESDAY
Moon Age Day 5   Moon Sign Leo

There is a good deal happening in relationships, not least of all where love is concerned. Even if you think that sort of thing is in the past for you, romance could come knocking on your door all the same. When it comes to getting things done in a general sense, tried and tested methods will probably work best.

31 WEDNESDAY
Moon Age Day 6   Moon Sign Leo

Trends suggest that you will be in the mood for spring cleaning today, and with a slightly ruthless streak about you at the moment you won't hold back when it comes to getting rid of things you genuinely don't need any more. Talk to relatives before you make drastic changes at home, though, or you could upset someone.

June

2017

1 THURSDAY
Moon Age Day 7   Moon Sign Virgo

This is a time for revitalising elements of your personal life and for getting them going in a direction that suits you. Clear the decks for new action in a practical sense and don't be in the least surprised if you discover that you are doing most of the work today. It isn't forced upon you – you choose it.

2 FRIDAY
Moon Age Day 8   Moon Sign Virgo

Career matters could prove to be a test of your patience, though probably not for long today. You are able to make a good impression on the world at large and will go to great lengths in order to show the world what you are made of. The competitive elements in your nature are truly on display now.

3 SATURDAY
Moon Age Day 9   Moon Sign Virgo

There could be a few disagreements to overcome right now and it might be suggested that getting involved in arguments in the first place is something of a waste of time. You would be better advised to go to almost any lengths to keep the peace. This will probably mean biting your tongue, something that doesn't come easily to a Scorpio.

4 SUNDAY
Moon Age Day 10   Moon Sign Libra

Getting around socially is what keeps a very definite smile on your face this Sunday. The chances are that you can afford to devote at least part of the day to having fun, and with the summer weather blossoming the prospect is all the more appealing. Get out of doors and into the fresh air. It's certain to do you good.

5 MONDAY
Moon Age Day 11   Moon Sign Libra

This turns out to be a wonderful period for all manner of intimate matters. Speaking candidly to your nearest and dearest won't be at all difficult and affairs of the heart can be honestly addressed now. Routines won't interest you very much and practical skills could be on hold for today.

6 TUESDAY
Moon Age Day 12   Moon Sign Scorpio

This is a time for making tracks and for pushing ahead with projects that please you. Leave the dross alone for a couple of days because the lunar high demands you make advances in your life. Any tiredness that could have been around for a few days now blows away on a breeze of optimism.

7 WEDNESDAY
Moon Age Day 13   Moon Sign Scorpio

The lunar high continues and your luck is in today, so don't be frightened to take the odd well-thought-out chance. Most of them will be well considered in any case and you are clearly very astute now. The sarcastic side of Scorpio is not in evidence this week, which partly explains the even greater level of popularity you are presently enjoying.

8 THURSDAY
Moon Age Day 14   Moon Sign Sagittarius

There might be some ups and downs in finances, a fact that you will have to address at some stage during today. In other respects life ticks along in a fairly routine way, that is unless you are willing to put in that extra bit of effort that can really bring results. Social prospects can also be good if you put in a little effort.

9 FRIDAY
Moon Age Day 15   Moon Sign Sagittarius

Family matters are on your mind and talking things through can help. What you don't need in any situation at the moment is to clam up and refuse to speak your mind. Not everything you have to say will be agreed with but at least you will have the satisfaction of knowing that you tried.

10 SATURDAY   *Moon Age Day 16   Moon Sign Sagittarius*

Firming up financial matters is made easy with co-operation and a little extra thought on your part. Avoid doing too much that others would see as interfering because it is not difficult to find yourself on the wrong side of certain individuals at this time. Arrange to do something very different in the evening.

11 SUNDAY   *Moon Age Day 17   Moon Sign Capricorn*

Not everything on your personal agenda can be completed quite as quickly or efficiently as you might wish today. That means being willing to sort through the necessary matters and dealing with what is truly important. In any case you will want at least some hours to spend with loved ones.

12 MONDAY   *Moon Age Day 18   Moon Sign Capricorn*

Attending to a variety of tasks will not be at all hard at the beginning of this working week. You look at life with a very practised eye and would be hardly likely to come up against problems that you fail to address successfully. At work you may find that you not only do your own work, but some rightfully belonging to others too.

13 TUESDAY   *Moon Age Day 19   Moon Sign Aquarius*

Social and romantic matters should prove especially interesting today. It appears that in some respects you have taken on a new lease of life. There are people around who you find particularly interesting and there is plenty to keep you occupied in a social sense. This would be an ideal time to ask an important question.

14 WEDNESDAY   *Moon Age Day 20   Moon Sign Aquarius*

You could do worse today than to take off to somewhere different. There are plenty of possibilities and the more you think about it, the greater are your options. The only slight problem if you stick around is that you will try to do everything at once, a course of action that is very likely to lead to exhaustion.

15 THURSDAY *Moon Age Day 21   Moon Sign Aquarius*

Career prospects are very good and you need to show what you are made of to superiors. If you are offered new responsibilities you should not turn these down out of hand. Having confidence in your own abilities is what today is all about and there are gains to be made if you ask the right questions.

16 FRIDAY *Moon Age Day 22   Moon Sign Pisces*

Parts of your inner life are now open to review. There are chinks in your armour, through which people can gain a much better understanding of what actually makes you tick. Although this isn't the most comfortable situation as far as you are concerned, it is very illuminating to the world at large.

17 SATURDAY *Moon Age Day 23   Moon Sign Pisces*

You seem to be the life and soul of the party now and will be having a good time at any social event that takes place this weekend. All the time you grow in confidence and feel yourself to be getting to destinations that would have seemed impossible once upon a time. You can afford to gloat a little but there is still much to be done.

18 SUNDAY *Moon Age Day 24   Moon Sign Aries*

A variety of interests now assist you in getting the very most out of your life in a holistic sense. After a slightly different sort of day yesterday, the gentler side of your nature is now on display. Finding ways to fill your time should not be at all difficult right now, at least not if your friends have anything to do with it.

19 MONDAY *Moon Age Day 25   Moon Sign Aries*

You are now entering a transitional period, during which it is sometimes difficult to see the road ahead quite as clearly as you would wish. It is going to take some time to rationalise everything that is going on in your life in quite the way you would wish. Be patient and everything will resolve itself fully eventually.

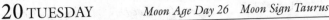

20 TUESDAY   *Moon Age Day 26   Moon Sign Taurus*

Not the best day of the month, all things considered. The monthly lunar low means that you will be lacking in both energy and confidence. The best way to deal with today is to relax and to seek the sort of fun that doesn't rely on running yourself ragged. If the weather is good enough, you need to find a deckchair and sit in it.

21 WEDNESDAY   *Moon Age Day 27   Moon Sign Taurus*

Take one job at a time and don't expect to rush ahead at this stage of the working week. Once again, you would respond very well to some rest, though that might be difficult on a working day. Allow others to make some of the running and seek out the right solution to a few small problems.

22 THURSDAY   *Moon Age Day 28   Moon Sign Gemini*

You should opt for a complete change if you can, mostly of scenery. Staying in the same place is likely to bore you and meanwhile, the more competitive and sporting side of your nature is on display. Most important of all, you simply want to enjoy yourself and can help others to do the same.

23 FRIDAY   *Moon Age Day 29   Moon Sign Gemini*

If you are considering a long journey today, or indeed in the near future, it should prove to be quite fortunate. The Sun is now entering your solar ninth house, bringing a change in emphasis and probably also in pace. Scorpios who have planned a holiday now should find it very successful. Happy news may be coming to you from a distant place.

24 SATURDAY   *Moon Age Day 0   Moon Sign Cancer*

Moneymaking opportunities should not be ignored this weekend. Maybe you have an idea for increasing your income that you know to be sound and all you need is a trustworthy ally. Whatever comes into your mind around now is worth considering, so talk it over with someone you know well and rate highly.

25 SUNDAY
Moon Age Day 1   Moon Sign Cancer

Sunday brings further possibilities in terms of travel and ideal opportunities to get some fresh air and exercise. If you are a sporting Scorpio, you may be donning your shorts and competing in some way, though no matter what your proclivities, you get a better chance to enjoy yourself when away from routines.

26 MONDAY
Moon Age Day 2   Moon Sign Leo

Look out for pressures coming from above. It is true that you have the ability to get on well in a practical sense, but that won't necessarily please everyone. The way to deal with such eventualities is to be diplomatic. No amount of arguing is going to get you what you want now so instead accept that you need to be flexible in your attitude.

27 TUESDAY
Moon Age Day 3   Moon Sign Leo

You can benefit greatly from having something new and interesting to do today. Forget the usual Tuesday routines. Even though it is entirely possible that you will have to toe the line during working hours, once the whistle goes your time is your own. With plenty of energy, you might decide on some form of exercise or other leisure activity.

28 WEDNESDAY
Moon Age Day 4   Moon Sign Leo

It is likely that today will find you looking carefully at existing relationships, which are quite promising around now. There is a lot of emotional support present, even if the majority of it is coming from your direction. Don't be too quick to criticise someone who is doing something in a way you wouldn't. It takes all sorts!

29 THURSDAY
Moon Age Day 5   Moon Sign Virgo

You are supported by a whole host of people and will probably be enjoying life immensely. Relationships are especially good at this time and you can probably feel closer to some individuals than has been the case for ages. What matters most right now is that you feel basically good inside.

30 FRIDAY
Moon Age Day 6   Moon Sign Virgo

You can expect the planets to place a positive influence over some of your deep-seated ambitions at this time. There is good potential for advancement at present, especially in your professional life. If you are a student, now is the time to apply maximum effort in order to get the results that your recent hard work deserves.

July

2017

1 SATURDAY
Moon Age Day 7   Moon Sign Libra

Current planetary trends should keep you happily involved in plans and schemes that you have been putting together of late. Don't let it worry you if you feel that not everyone is interested in what you have to say at the moment. The most important thing is to focus on what your ultimate dream really is, and then to go for it.

2 SUNDAY
Moon Age Day 8   Moon Sign Libra

Right now travel and cultural pursuits are once again on your mind. You may find that you are choosing to put yourself out in the wider world, which should make life especially interesting on a summer Sunday. Long journeys are a possibility for some Scorpios now and you may find that the further you can go, the better the fun.

3 MONDAY
Moon Age Day 9   Moon Sign Scorpio

A plan that has been up in the air for quite some time now looks as though it will begin to work out well for you. The Moon is in your sign bringing you a good opportunity to test your general luck. Although you may find one or two friends difficult to deal with, in the main people should be co-operative and happy to follow your lead.

4 TUESDAY
Moon Age Day 10   Moon Sign Scorpio

The lunar high continues and you are raring to have a good time. If work curtails your intention to find excitement, either take a day's holiday or else confine your activities to later in the day. With so much to play for it seems that you can hardly put a foot wrong. Even people who haven't liked you before may do so now.

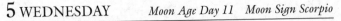

5 WEDNESDAY   *Moon Age Day 11   Moon Sign Scorpio*

Getting to grips with certain serious issues is more or less certain to take up at least a part of your day. Don't allow such issues to get in the way of your natural enjoyment of the day in a social sense. You need to be mixing as freely as you can at the moment and with as many different types of people as possible.

6 THURSDAY   *Moon Age Day 12   Moon Sign Sagittarius*

Getting out and about socially or undertaking new intellectual interests is what today seems to be all about. You shouldn't have to try very hard when it comes to the new or the unusual because these things will find their way to your door. Curb your natural enthusiasm if it could mean getting into a dangerous situation.

7 FRIDAY   *Moon Age Day 13   Moon Sign Sagittarius*

There could be something happening to you professionally that offers a signpost towards future successes. Keep all options open and avoid getting bogged down too much with routines at this time. Conferences or even simple conversations can teach you a great deal more about the way your own mind is actually working.

8 SATURDAY   *Moon Age Day 14   Moon Sign Capricorn*

Your love life could offer pause for thought as you try to work out what is going through the mind of your partner. If you don't have one, then your curiosity might turn instead in the direction of family members and possibly even a very good friend. Working out what makes people tick is half the fun you get from today.

9 SUNDAY   *Moon Age Day 15   Moon Sign Capricorn*

It may be obvious now that you have to rethink a plan of action in order to increase general progress in your life. Efficiency and improved organisation would help but these might be out of the window on account of general responsibilities towards those around you. Keep up your efforts to get out and about more if you can today.

10 MONDAY *Moon Age Day 16* *Moon Sign Capricorn*

Challenges may arise today, along with situations that test your ability and progressive qualities. In the main these should be welcome and are likely to find you performing extremely well, even at new tasks. There is a greater degree of self-assurance around and an ability to move obstacles that seemed impossible before.

11 TUESDAY *Moon Age Day 17* *Moon Sign Aquarius*

You seem to be enjoying quite a high profile at the moment. People coming and going in your life will take more notice of your presence and you will regularly be sought out for advice. At work you are likely to be quite active, and probably passing on your pearls of wisdom to important people.

12 WEDNESDAY *Moon Age Day 18* *Moon Sign Aquarius*

There will still be a great deal happening in your life, but is much of it what you really want? Maybe you should think carefully today about incentives that are already underway or else planned. It is possible that you are doing a lot but actually achieving very little that you find personally pleasing.

13 THURSDAY *Moon Age Day 19* *Moon Sign Pisces*

It might seem particularly exciting to seek out new social contacts at this time. The middle of July could be quite inspirational in some ways, particularly with new options on offer. Now the summer is truly here and there's a good chance that the restless side of your nature is beginning to show, put your thoughts and ideas into practice and make some phone calls!

14 FRIDAY *Moon Age Day 20* *Moon Sign Pisces*

No matter how well you plan for today, confusion is liable to follow. Invariably this will be down to the actions of others and not a direct response to anything you are doing yourself. Remain patient and enjoy what the altered circumstances bring. It's simply a matter of remaining optimistic in every situation.

15 SATURDAY
Moon Age Day 21   Moon Sign Aries

You could do far worse this weekend than to get away from it all. You won't especially want to be with strangers but can gain a great deal from more intimate or family relationships. There is a competitive side to your nature when it comes to sporting activities, which may seem attractive today.

16 SUNDAY
Moon Age Day 22   Moon Sign Aries

Freedom is the key to happiness, which is why so many Scorpios will be choosing this time for holidays. If that isn't possible, perhaps broaden your horizons in some other way. Take some time out to do something that really interests you and which will turn your mind away from your worries. Travel may broaden the mind, but any space and fresh air works wonders.

17 MONDAY
Moon Age Day 23   Moon Sign Aries

Trends move on and today you should be enjoying fun on the home front a great deal more than has been the case recently. More willing to settle and less inclined to be gadding about all the time you are certainly keen to get to know loved ones even better. Romantic overtones are also present in intimate relationships today.

18 TUESDAY
Moon Age Day 24   Moon Sign Taurus

A go-slow policy now seems to be in operation. Don't allow yourself to get depressed just because the lunar low is around. In a couple of days you will be back to your own vibrant self. In the meantime you will simply have to come to terms with a slower pace and take more time to think.

19 WEDNESDAY
Moon Age Day 25   Moon Sign Taurus

Present circumstances predict another quiet day and one during which you can make more of personal relationships. Spend time with family members and do something that interests you in a quiet way. If you are at work today you should get the chance to consolidate on some recent positive actions and make some quiet achievements.

20 THURSDAY   *Moon Age Day 26   Moon Sign Gemini*

Professionally speaking, you are able to make the best of the Sun, which is still just in your tenth house at the moment. It stays there until after tomorrow, allowing you to get ahead in a number of different ways. You should find others willing to rely on you and able to offer more in the way of rewards.

21 FRIDAY   *Moon Age Day 27   Moon Sign Gemini*

There are limitations to contend with, though a few of them you will barely notice. It's important to keep busy today, but not to bite off more than you can chew. Social trends remain good and you will be happiest of all when you are in the company of people who have always had the ability to make you laugh.

22 SATURDAY   *Moon Age Day 28   Moon Sign Cancer*

You have to work pretty hard for anything you really want today but that fact is not likely to worry you too much. With energy to spare, and the sort of determination that few can better, you are likely to make a splash. This would be another ideal time for Scorpio to be thinking about a holiday.

23 SUNDAY   *Moon Age Day 0   Moon Sign Cancer*

A broadening of mental horizons can be expected today, together with a greater than usual willingness to tell those around you how you really feel about certain matters. Coming clean improves your general mood and it also means that friends and relatives alike have a better understanding of what really makes you tick.

24 MONDAY   *Moon Age Day 1   Moon Sign Leo*

You can expect a good start to the working week. Be willing to put yourself out to help others, especially people you know to be deserving of your effort and time. In a social sense, you are likely to be quite jolly and up for a laugh. Don't be surprised if some extra attention is coming your way.

25 TUESDAY   *Moon Age Day 2   Moon Sign Leo*

You may feel a strong urge to enjoy your personal freedom and make the most of it right now, which is not really all that unusual for the zodiac sign of Scorpio. If any sort of dispute should happen to arise, you are about to learn who your friends are. Some of them come from places that are really going to surprise you today.

26 WEDNESDAY   *Moon Age Day 3   Moon Sign Virgo*

Expect to encounter some genuine opposition today, most likely with regard to plans you want to put into action. If you occupy any sort of public position, the flack will naturally be that much harder to avoid. With too little time to do everything you want, it is necessary to think clearly and be quite selective regarding your efforts.

27 THURSDAY   *Moon Age Day 4   Moon Sign Virgo*

Something seems to be missing from your life today. Perhaps it is the company of certain family members, or friends who are away for the moment. Trends suggest that you will have to rely quite heavily on your own opinions without the support of others, though this experience does you a great deal of good in the longer-term and is apt to strengthen your convictions.

28 FRIDAY   *Moon Age Day 5   Moon Sign Libra*

Things generally are going your way but you are a very political animal at present and so can still find yourself on the wrong side of the opinions put forward by others. It can sometimes feel as though you are being criticised, no matter what you decide to do. Take no notice because at least you pitch in and try.

29 SATURDAY   *Moon Age Day 6   Moon Sign Libra*

There is now a focus on finances, and a need to curb your spending somewhat. It isn't that you are poverty stricken, merely that you want to save for something important, perhaps a break or a much-needed holiday. In a way, it doesn't matter because enjoying yourself at the moment is likely to cost you nothing.

30 SUNDAY *Moon Age Day 7   Moon Sign Libra*

This is a go ahead time in almost every way, even if it takes you some time to get fully into gear on this summer Sunday. It could be that you feel you have pushed hard enough during the week. If so, all you will want to do now is relax. If you manage to do so while still taking some sort of physical or mental exercise, so much the better.

31 MONDAY *Moon Age Day 8   Moon Sign Scorpio*

You ought to be looking and feeling at your best right now. Make the most of this Monday by pleasing yourself. That doesn't mean, however, that you should be ignoring others. On the contrary, you seem to have time for the whole world and make friends wherever you go. This is really Scorpio at its best.

August 2017

1 TUESDAY
Moon Age Day 9   Moon Sign Scorpio

Seek out the assistance of people you know can do you some good. It doesn't really matter if these are individuals you might have feared in the past because right now you are game enough to talk to anyone. The sheer scale of your potential successes at the moment might surprise you most of all.

2 WEDNESDAY
Moon Age Day 10   Moon Sign Sagittarius

Your ego might be well and truly boosted today, as much as anything by the remarks others are making towards you. Although there are ongoing jobs and tasks that have to be done, in some ways you are taking a refreshingly new look at life. As a result, rearrangements are much more likely at this time.

3 THURSDAY
Moon Age Day 11   Moon Sign Sagittarius

You feel the need to put back some of the spice of life that has seemed to be missing. You can do this with your romantic partner, or on a general social level, though it is hard to achieve at work. What won't be too easy is to split your time successfully. Present trends show situations becoming intermingled and confused.

4 FRIDAY
Moon Age Day 12   Moon Sign Sagittarius

It might be best today to only take on tasks you know you are both good at and can complete. The frustration that is around comes from a feeling that you are either restricted or totally stopped in your tracks. Take time to make the right decisions in the first place and then this should not be a problem at all.

5 SATURDAY
Moon Age Day 13   Moon Sign Capricorn

Your desire for intimacy around now is well catered for at home with your partner, but you might also feel a new sort of closeness when in the company of friends. Could it be that those you meet are opening up more, or might it be you who is somehow different? Think this through carefully, as this is a question only you can answer.

6 SUNDAY
Moon Age Day 14   Moon Sign Capricorn

Try to introduce some variety into your routines as much as you can today. The winds of change have begun to blow, but you need to give them a push. People you know could prove to be rather more exciting today than of late, though most of them will be responding to what they see as an alteration of attitude and enthusiasm within yourself.

7 MONDAY
Moon Age Day 15   Moon Sign Aquarius

Slowly but surely, life is moving onward and upward, beginning to achieve a pace and a vitality that may have been somewhat lacking so far this month. You need to pace yourself but not too much. Discussions also bring a delicate balance, this time between putting forward your own opinion and yet remaining fair.

8 TUESDAY
Moon Age Day 16   Moon Sign Aquarius

This continues to be a favourable period in most respects, though less so if you take life too seriously. It has to be said that Scorpio is not the natural comic of the zodiac but you do possess a rather black sense of humour, with a dryness that others appreciate. You won't be everyone's cup of tea today but that would be impossible anyway.

9 WEDNESDAY
Moon Age Day 17   Moon Sign Pisces

There are good things happening today and you can be part of them. It really depends on your state of mind from the very start of the day. It would be sensible to take an optimistic view because what you project at the moment has a great bearing on the way life answers you. Think big and big things should come to you!

10 THURSDAY   *Moon Age Day 18   Moon Sign Pisces*

Travel issues should be helped to go your way with a few timely communications. Quite a few Scorpio people will be on holiday at this time, or else planning to go away very soon. If you are one of them, the auspices are extremely good. Monetary matters need some careful thought and a bit of prior planning, though.

11 FRIDAY   *Moon Age Day 19   Moon Sign Pisces*

This is a period when you can capitalise on the chance to do something unusual or different. If you are somewhat uncomfortable, perhaps because of an old war wound, it would be best to keep busy at this time. Putting things to the back of your mind appears to become an art form for Scorpio around now.

12 SATURDAY   *Moon Age Day 20   Moon Sign Aries*

There are influences about that put you in touch with the wider social world now. Conformation of something you suspected may be coming along later in the day, though you might have to concentrate on what others are saying to realise it. You remain busy, generally happy and quite keen to make some sort of splash.

13 SUNDAY   ☿   *Moon Age Day 21   Moon Sign Aries*

This is another of those periods when you find it quite easy to deal with several jobs at the same time. Don't be too willing to take on board the problems of the world though. It's true that you almost always want to be of assistance but at the end of the day you can't live the lives of others for them.

14 MONDAY   ☿   *Moon Age Day 22   Moon Sign Taurus*

Keep things simple today and don't try too hard. The lunar low this time around should not prevent you from enjoying life to the full, but if you try to complicate matters you could come unstuck. Attitude is all-important, particularly when you are dealing with especially sensitive people.

15 TUESDAY ☿ *Moon Age Day 23   Moon Sign Taurus*

Certain delays may be inevitable today. All the same you should notice the lunar low less this month than at any stage this year. The reason for this is a strong planetary line-up that helps you through difficulties and keeps you feeling generally confident. Stay away from awkward people and avoid responsibilities you don't want.

16 WEDNESDAY ☿ *Moon Age Day 24   Moon Sign Gemini*

There could be a good deal of impatience coming from your direction today if you find yourself tied down by too many obligations. What really appeals is to be free to do whatever you wish, as much as possible. Where family gatherings are concerned you should find yourself to be the life and soul of the party.

17 THURSDAY ☿ *Moon Age Day 25   Moon Sign Gemini*

The right company should definitely assist you to get ahead now. The more you give out to the world at large, the greater are the benefits that come back to you. Don't get tied down with pointless or irritating details at work or at home and use this day to please others, as well as to make yourself happier on the way.

18 FRIDAY ☿ *Moon Age Day 26   Moon Sign Cancer*

Make the most of career opportunities now and get ahead of tasks before they become due. With masses of energy, and a real determination to fill every available minute with activity, there is very little to hold you back. What you do have to remember is that it is quite possible to run yourself ragged, so take some time out occasionally.

19 SATURDAY ☿ *Moon Age Day 27   Moon Sign Cancer*

Positive social highlights are on the cards for today, but they might slow you down somewhat in a practical sense. Keep abreast of news and views, taking in everything that those around you are saying at this time. Even the most inane gossip can prove to be important to you in the days ahead.

20 SUNDAY ☿ *Moon Age Day 28 Moon Sign Leo*

When it comes to your personal life there appears to be no trouble making things work today. This is a Sunday that could prove to be very important in the widest sense because you have it in your power to institute changes now that last for a long time. Keeping a sense of proportion might be quite impossible for today.

21 MONDAY ☿ *Moon Age Day 29 Moon Sign Leo*

You should have little difficulty finding out exactly what interests you at the moment. Once you have done so you tend to march forward confidently towards a more certain future. Although you may have quite a lot on your plate in terms of work, in a general sense you are happy to take on new tasks too.

22 TUESDAY ☿ *Moon Age Day 0 Moon Sign Virgo*

Career-wise it looks as though you are still heading in the right direction. Take the chance that today offers to break with routine and to tell people how things should be done. It's important to remain diplomatic and not to turn people against you who might be most useful later on.

23 WEDNESDAY ☿ *Moon Age Day 1 Moon Sign Virgo*

The Sun is now in your solar eleventh house, bringing a new period during which you do much to enhance your social and personal life. Are you really taking more notice of the people who figure in your life or does it just seem that way? Certainly the response you get from those around you will be gratifying.

24 THURSDAY ☿ *Moon Age Day 2 Moon Sign Virgo*

Your fortunes as far as friendship is concerned seem to be on the up. There are new people about to come into your life, probably as acquaintances first of all, but later as friends. This proves to be important because Scorpio tends to keep its friends for many years, forming often deep attachments. Good times lie ahead of you.

25 FRIDAY ☿ *Moon Age Day 3   Moon Sign Libra*

Having worked steadily towards some of your recent objectives, it appears that you are now in a position to reap the benefits. Most Scorpios will already have the weekend in view and will be keen to socialise as soon as work is out of the way. Make the most of these trends, even if you are rather tired as it won't be long before you perk up again.

26 SATURDAY ☿ *Moon Age Day 4   Moon Sign Libra*

Whilst you might enjoy being the team leader today, you will have to face some sort of opposition. Never mind, you're in fighting form and won't back down just because of a little criticism. Stick to your Scorpio guns, whilst at the same time remain always willing to concede the odd point when you know you are wrong.

27 SUNDAY ☿ *Moon Age Day 5   Moon Sign Scorpio*

Now you make the best of all types of social encounters. There could even be some romantic interest coming into your life if you are a young or single Scorpio. Family pleasures are possible but you get even more today from mixing with friends. There are plenty of laughs about and you are creating a few of them.

28 MONDAY ☿ *Moon Age Day 6   Moon Sign Scorpio*

There are some very lucky influences around at the moment. The Moon is back in your sign and means that you have plenty of energy, and no lack of ideas regarding the way you use it. At both work and home you should be on good form, anxious to make an excellent impression and keen to get on with life.

29 TUESDAY ☿ *Moon Age Day 7   Moon Sign Sagittarius*

Socially speaking you are probably on the up and up today. This part of the working week finds you anxious to be in good company and probably very excited by at least some of the prospects that are around now. Once again you gain from travel and lose out if you are tied to the same spot for more than a few hours.

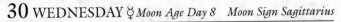

30 WEDNESDAY ☿ *Moon Age Day 8   Moon Sign Sagittarius*

You may simply try to accomplish too much at this time, which is why a little rest and relaxation could be quite welcome on this high summer Wednesday. Keep a sense of proportion in your dealings with loved ones, some of whom might be having the odd problem. A sense of freedom is still all-important.

31 THURSDAY ☿ *Moon Age Day 9   Moon Sign Sagittarius*

You may need to look at a recent project again. Perhaps because of some faulty planning in the first place, it would be sensible to start from scratch. Far from being a chore this will almost certainly turn out to be a labour of love. Do a little of this and a bit of that today - in order to keep life balanced.

September 2017

1 FRIDAY
☿ Moon Age Day 10   Moon Sign Capricorn

Stand by for a period during which you will find yourself interacting with all manner of different people. Although socially you tend to be best with people you know, the more adventurous side of your zodiac sign is now also on display. Set to doing things bright and early this morning and keep up your efforts.

2 SATURDAY
☿ Moon Age Day 11   Moon Sign Capricorn

Lack of organisation could cause a major plan to hit the buffers today. Before you embark on any task, make very sure that you have all the facts and figures that you need to hand and be bold in your desire to get ahead. There is plenty of help and support around when you need it the most, even if you have to search to find it.

3 SUNDAY
☿ Moon Age Day 12   Moon Sign Aquarius

Trends suggest that you might be in something of an impetuous mood this Sunday. There's nothing at all wrong with this, just as long as you don't go off the deep end. Keep your enthusiasm under some sort of wraps and be careful not to give unintentional offence. Your creative potential should be especially good now.

4 MONDAY
☿ Moon Age Day 13   Moon Sign Aquarius

Much more harmonious social and romantic encounters are now likely to be coming your way. With a fine sense of balance you are less likely to cause offence to others and have exactly what it takes to be very popular amongst your friends. Many of them may even look to you for a special sort of inspiration.

5 TUESDAY ☿ *Moon Age Day 14 Moon Sign Aquarius*

There is such a strong planetary influence on the social scene right now that it seems unlikely you could avoid being overtaken by it. Chatting away, ten to the dozen, you are probably the most talkative Scorpio you have been all year. Most aspects of life prove to be steady, leaving time to simply have fun.

6 WEDNESDAY ☿ *Moon Age Day 15 Moon Sign Pisces*

Today's trends indicate that you may have to pay serious attention now to financial matters. This is one area of life that doesn't fascinate you very much at present. Short of winning the lottery, though, it is something you must address. Talk things through with loved ones and think of ingenious ways to get more cash flowing.

7 THURSDAY ☿ *Moon Age Day 16 Moon Sign Pisces*

Where your love life is concerned you are certainly likely to have had better days than this. Since you cannot do too much about this situation, it would be better to concentrate on friendship instead. Be circumspect in your dealings with people you don't know very well, though maybe more trusting than you usually are.

8 FRIDAY ☿ *Moon Age Day 17 Moon Sign Aries*

Certain obligations you feel to others will chafe somewhat today. Grit your teeth and get on with them. Once this situation is out of the way you can then get on with enjoying yourself again. If further duties beckon later in the day, try to delay them for a while. You definitely shouldn't allow yourself to become depressed today.

9 SATURDAY ☿ *Moon Age Day 18 Moon Sign Aries*

With a slight lack of confidence in yourself today, together with a fairly absent-minded phase, it may seem that you are taking two steps forward and three back. It won't be long before you get yourself fully into the swing of things but in the meantime you will have to rely on intuition.

10 SUNDAY ☿ *Moon Age Day 19   Moon Sign Taurus*

This may not be the very best period of the month, especially for making progress or getting on with specific tasks. The regular monthly lunar low saps some of your energy but it does little to have a bearing on your social impulses. Stay around people you know and remain absolutely determined to have some fun.

11 MONDAY ☿ *Moon Age Day 20   Moon Sign Taurus*

This is likely to be another fairly sluggish day and probably won't offer you a great deal of what you are looking for in life at this time. Never mind. You can rely on other people to help you out whenever necessary and should still be enjoying what life has to offer on a social and personal footing. Take comfort from the fact that this is just a temporary lull.

12 TUESDAY ☿ *Moon Age Day 21   Moon Sign Gemini*

Professionally speaking you can expect a more progressive phase to come along now. Some of your ambitions might appear to have a greater chance of success and you should be able to find the help you have been looking for in a specific direction. Also, if you are out shopping today you should keep your eyes open for a bargain.

13 WEDNESDAY *Moon Age Day 22   Moon Sign Gemini*

In terms of the competitive side of life you might not feel you are making very much progress. Things will soon change, especially if you adopt a different way of looking at old problems. However, since you have plenty of vitality today it appears that you can get a great deal done in a practical sense.

14 THURSDAY *Moon Age Day 23   Moon Sign Cancer*

Trends strike a warning note today: you could end up in some sort of undesirable situation if you put too much trust in certain other people. It would probably be best to trust in yourself alone for the moment and also being prepared to make important decisions without relying on others. Concern for specific family members might be unjustified.

15 FRIDAY *Moon Age Day 24 Moon Sign Cancer*

Try a variety of tasks and interests today because you are feeling more flexible and quite capable. Success definitely comes through diversity as far as you are concerned and you can also gain at the moment by simply keeping your eyes and ears open. Personally speaking you might find you have a secret admirer.

16 SATURDAY *Moon Age Day 25 Moon Sign Cancer*

Domestic situations can be quite demanding, leaving you feeling that there isn't much of Saturday left for you to spend doing what naturally appeals to you. However, confidence is present and you are likely to find plenty to make you smile, both at home and out there in the wider world.

17 SUNDAY *Moon Age Day 26 Moon Sign Leo*

There can be tiresome aspects to today, particularly in terms of friendship. Maybe people are asking too much of you or putting you in a difficult position? Although planetary trends show that you are likely to keep your cool, you may be forced to show how you feel about the situation.

18 MONDAY *Moon Age Day 27 Moon Sign Leo*

With plenty of variety on offer, the chances of becoming bored today are not high. You might find that you need to concentrate on a few important issues and could be required to deal with at least one potentially thorny problem relating to your partner. Money matters may also require some inventive thought.

19 TUESDAY *Moon Age Day 28 Moon Sign Virgo*

This might turn out to be the best period during September for getting new initiatives started. These require a good deal of planning, most of which has probably already been undertaken. All that remains is to decide upon strategy, something that you are particularly good at under present planetary trends.

20 WEDNESDAY
Moon Age Day 0   Moon Sign Virgo

There are favourable highlights shining on group activities today. The loner inside Scorpio is certainly taking a holiday and you should be operating extremely well in a team, at least for the present. Strong social trends predominate, so the chances are that you are doing things that please you, rather than jobs that feed you.

21 THURSDAY
Moon Age Day 1   Moon Sign Libra

A mental peak continues, offering a Thursday that is big on success but probably less geared towards practical matters. Use your intuition because it is particularly strong at the present time. Assessing the likely actions or reactions of those around you ought to be child's play for most of today.

22 FRIDAY
Moon Age Day 2   Moon Sign Libra

You should enjoy a degree of freedom today, thinking and doing whatever you wish. Maybe someone who is often on your back is away at present, or it could simply be that you are taking matters into your own hands. Since your creative potential is also good you should turn your hand to art, or perhaps some redecoration at home?

23 SATURDAY
Moon Age Day 3   Moon Sign Scorpio

Things should be looking good today. The Moon is in your zodiac sign and as always during the lunar high there is everything to play for. You can look forward to better-than-average progress in all sorts of ways and should find that the necessary support to do what you wish is easy to come by. This is definitely not a time to hold back.

24 SUNDAY
Moon Age Day 4   Moon Sign Scorpio

This ought to be another generally promising day. Get out and about in the world if you have the chance to. Socially speaking you should be on top form and more than anxious to mix with as many different sorts of people as you can. This is definitely a time for making changes in your life, some of which could be far-reaching.

25 MONDAY *Moon Age Day 5   Moon Sign Scorpio*

Whilst you can sense that your domestic partner has your best interests at heart, you are unlikely to agree with the suggestions he or she is making. Trying to do your own thing, whilst at the same time remaining kind and tactful, won't be at all easy. The only way round the situation is to try to explain how you have reached your decisions.

26 TUESDAY *Moon Age Day 6   Moon Sign Sagittarius*

On a personal level, you could be having difficulties at work. Perhaps people misunderstand your motives or maybe they understand them all too well? You can put this situation right but it is going to take some thinking about. Don't be worried about taking some time out to rest if you feel really jaded at any stage today.

27 WEDNESDAY *Moon Age Day 7   Moon Sign Sagittarius*

A slightly tense atmosphere can prevail if you spend too much time trying to deal with emotional issues. The less you concentrate on specifics today, the better time you will have so keep things light and airy and avoid any deep heart-to-hearts. Your confidence is on the increase and Wednesday workers might be the potentially luckiest Scorpio people of all.

28 THURSDAY *Moon Age Day 8   Moon Sign Capricorn*

It is the little things in life that make things feel somewhat easier today. You are like a person crossing a stream but for you at present there are large and closely placed stepping-stones. You should notice this particularly in the workplace, probably because your social life is even more instinctive right now.

29 FRIDAY *Moon Age Day 9   Moon Sign Capricorn*

Yet more emphasis is now placed on favourable career issues. If you are still studying, you may notice that actually getting the necessary information into your head is that much easier at this time and there are few indications for any Scorpios of insurmountable difficulties around this period.

30 SATURDAY *Moon Age Day 10 Moon Sign Capricorn*

Friendship continues to be a source of joy as the weekend gets started. You may be slightly more hesitant than usual, particularly when it comes to making decisions you know to be of supreme importance, but you won't stick fast over personal or family issues. Listen to what you recognise to be sound advice.

October
2017

1 SUNDAY
Moon Age Day 11   Moon Sign Aquarius

Today you should feel freer to express yourself – in some cases perhaps too much so. Don't forget you are dealing with the feelings and emotions of those you care for the most. Being outspoken is all well and good but you shouldn't lose sight of your sense of responsibility. Stand by for new relationships to commence.

2 MONDAY
Moon Age Day 12   Moon Sign Aquarius

Apart from the happiness you are getting from personal relationships at the moment there isn't a great deal of sense that you are getting very far in the competitive world. Perhaps you need to give your more practical and professional life something of a boost? There are opportunities to do so if you keep looking.

3 TUESDAY
Moon Age Day 13   Moon Sign Pisces

Feeling yourself to be amongst just the right sort of company is what today is about. You are now more perceptive than usual and know where to go to get just the right sort of assistance. Where you really gain today, however, is in one-to-one relationships, especially with your partner. Romance is calling – can't you hear it?

4 WEDNESDAY
Moon Age Day 14   Moon Sign Pisces

The general routines of life could keep you busy today if you allow them to do so. If you want any change and diversity, you will have to go out and search for it. Favourable times are approaching in a financial sense and so take the time to look carefully at new ways of earning more money.

135

5 THURSDAY
Moon Age Day 15   Moon Sign Aries

A sense of team spirit could be lacking and that is part of what you have to put back into your life as soon as you can. There are people out there with whom you could really co-operate, plus a few individuals who have it in their power to boost your success rate. This is definitely a day to keep your eyes open.

6 FRIDAY
Moon Age Day 16   Moon Sign Aries

Although today is certainly not a time for grandiose plans, when it comes to the daily routines of life you appear to be getting on fine. However, you may soon notice that what is missing is excitement. Don't worry about this as the time isn't right for that yet and a few quieter days lie ahead. If you accept this fact you will enjoy today and the weekend more.

7 SATURDAY
Moon Age Day 17   Moon Sign Taurus

There is a possibility that you are even less enthusiastic than you intended to be today. All of a sudden it could feel as though everyone is relying solely on you and that is not a state of affairs you presently relish. Actually it's all a matter of perspective. In more positive times you would relish the attention.

8 SUNDAY
Moon Age Day 18   Moon Sign Taurus

The presence of the lunar low indicates that you should keep life as simple as possible this Sunday. Although the chilly winds might be on the way it wouldn't do any harm at all to get a little fresh air and a change of scene. Failing this, find some quiet and yet rewarding way to while away a few hours, possibly amongst family members.

9 MONDAY
Moon Age Day 19   Moon Sign Taurus

Make sure others don't get hold of the wrong end of the stick merely by explaining yourself carefully at present. Your attitude is one of armed neutrality at the moment, so others could find you to be somewhat aggressive. Settle down and spend some time with people you both like and trust.

10 TUESDAY   *Moon Age Day 20   Moon Sign Gemini*

The emphasis now sits squarely on having fun and being able to express yourself fully. Trends have moved on and some of the less favourable days of earlier in the month are gone and finished. Your attitude tends to be one of optimism, which is a big part of what you need to feel happy with your lot.

11 WEDNESDAY   *Moon Age Day 21   Moon Sign Gemini*

Your social environment contains more than a few interesting encounters that you would find particularly interesting during this midweek period. Some of these you are creating for yourself. This might be a favourable day to host a dinner party, or simply to go out in the evening with friends. Expect some admirers to gather round.

12 THURSDAY   *Moon Age Day 22   Moon Sign Cancer*

There is just a slight possibility that you will now be overlooking a number of details in your short and medium-term planning. Try to take a wider view and see the whole picture if you can and where you experience some difficulty, try to seek the support of others. Spread difficult tasks out across the day and don't overload yourself at any one time.

13 FRIDAY   *Moon Age Day 23   Moon Sign Cancer*

Your assessment of a personal situation could appear to be flawed in some way. The best time for thinking deeply about the more intimate aspects of your life would be in a few days from now. For today, it would seem to be sensible to adopt a casual attitude to life and to enjoy as much time with friends as you can manage.

14 SATURDAY   *Moon Age Day 24   Moon Sign Leo*

Along comes a good period for exploring different possibilities, plus the chance to do rather better in the financial stakes. The more change you bring into your life at this time, the sooner you will get out of the doldrums and back into the trade winds of life. Throw around a few compliments and see what happens.

15 SUNDAY
Moon Age Day 25   Moon Sign Leo

In terms of self-expression you are likely to be a good deal more ebullient right now than you usually are, which means exercising a little self-control if you don't want that Scorpio outspokenness to get you into trouble. Not everyone seems to be especially helpful and you can expect to have to work hard on your own behalf now.

16 MONDAY
Moon Age Day 26   Moon Sign Virgo

This should be a very good time for getting along with others, in almost any potential situation. Don't be too shy to put your point of view forward, even in situations that are not familiar to you. It is very unlikely that your opinions would be derided at the moment and, on the contrary, you could make new allies.

17 TUESDAY
Moon Age Day 27   Moon Sign Virgo

It looks as though this is a period during which you can spend some time thinking about personal matters that need special attention. With a slight pause in the general forward momentum of life and a contemplative mood coming upon you, fairly lengthy periods of concentrated pondering are indicated. Enjoy this small window of introspection.

18 WEDNESDAY
Moon Age Day 28   Moon Sign Libra

When it comes to most aspects of life at the moment, you appear to want to have your cake and eat it too. Who wouldn't, but it really isn't possible for most of the time. Be content with your lot, whilst at the same time hanging on to those aspirations for the future. Only remember that life doesn't owe any of us a living.

19 THURSDAY
Moon Age Day 29   Moon Sign Libra

There is plenty of scope for mutual assistance and a general sense of harmony now. Although you are still inclined to be somewhat pensive, you should also discover that your curiosity is raised significantly. This can lead to you digging and delving, which means more communication with the world in general.

20 FRIDAY
Moon Age Day 0   Moon Sign Libra

With less scope for influencing others today, you tend to retreat into your own little world again. There isn't really much alternative because the Moon is in your twelfth house, where your Sun is already residing. The results are temporary and certainly not negative, though friends might think you are down in the dumps.

21 SATURDAY
Moon Age Day 1   Moon Sign Scorpio

With the Moon moving back into your zodiac sign today you can expect a fairly active and generally quite helpful weekend. You may see this time as being your last big chance to do something grand before the winter sets in. If this is the case then you will want to spread your wings. Do so in the company of those you really like.

22 SUNDAY
Moon Age Day 2   Moon Sign Scorpio

This Sunday looks dynamic and very interesting. It's time to push your way to the front of the queue. This doesn't mean having to fall out with anyone but merely expresses your present desire to get things done in the least complicated manner. Your creative potential should also be especially good.

23 MONDAY
Moon Age Day 3   Moon Sign Sagittarius

This is a time for staying on the move, something you will certainly enjoy now. Don't allow yourself to be held back, especially at those times when you have made up your mind to a particular course of action. Messy jobs, or those that you simply don't fancy, are likely to be delegated with ease today while you move on to more attractive tasks.

24 TUESDAY
Moon Age Day 4   Moon Sign Sagittarius

A boost to all matters associated with communication comes along and you feel the wind of change blowing. Get on with jobs that have been waiting for a while and don't allow yourself to be restricted by people who have a vested interest in holding you back. The charitable side of your nature is on display now.

25 WEDNESDAY   *Moon Age Day 5   Moon Sign Sagittarius*

There may not be many opportunities to have your ego massaged today but you simply have to get on and do things all the same. There could be difficulty in deciding how you want to spend your free time, especially during a period when practically everyone in the family is trying to attract your attention.

26 THURSDAY   *Moon Age Day 6   Moon Sign Capricorn*

A phase of dynamism and activity is at hand. Go for gold today and make certain that absolutely everyone knows who you are and what you want from life. Your chart today reveals that you are entertaining, keen to talk to almost anyone and anxious to let the world know what you believe about a host of issues.

27 FRIDAY   *Moon Age Day 7   Moon Sign Capricorn*

It should be possible, if not easy, to make some really good progress today, especially if you are at work. In other areas, friends might appear distant, or even awkward, which could lead to you having to analyse their possible problems. Fortunately, your tolerance level is extremely high at the present time, as is your desire to help.

28 SATURDAY   *Moon Age Day 8   Moon Sign Aquarius*

Emotional relationships are potentially good, but there is a danger that they could be beset by a few misunderstandings. It is very important to make sure that your partner or others you care about deeply understand you. This ought to pose no real problem because your powers of communication are extremely good now.

29 SUNDAY   *Moon Age Day 9   Moon Sign Aquarius*

This Sunday marks a high-spirited period and one during which you are laying down a few plans for later in the week. A few of the slightly negative planetary positions of recent times are now disappearing, so it could feel as if you have been released from a sort of straightjacket. Socially, it's time to rock.

30 MONDAY
Moon Age Day 10   Moon Sign Pisces

News you might have been expecting regarding a personal matter could fail to materialise. If so, you will simply have to show how patient you can be and it should come along in due course. Be sure to keep confidences because you won't be thought of any better if it appears that you are giving away the secrets of a friend.

31 TUESDAY
Moon Age Day 11   Moon Sign Pisces

There could be some unaccountable mishaps at home, which you will want to deal with as quickly as possible. Don't get strung up today with details but concentrate instead on the matter at hand. In work situations you tend to give a good account of yourself and it is possible that you could make some new allies.

November
2017

1 WEDNESDAY
Moon Age Day 12   Moon Sign Pisces

Now the temptation to empty your pocket on expensive things that you don't require could be quite strong. Before every proposed purchase stop and think carefully and then decide whether this is something you actually do need. As a result of some more positive trends, there could be some startling new ideas around now and you will want to go for them all.

2 THURSDAY
Moon Age Day 13   Moon Sign Aries

Show some patience, particularly with regard to people who can be irritating in the extreme. It won't help to lose your temper but it would be very good indeed if, instead, you could find people marvelling at your tolerance. Try to keep away from meaningless and boring routines if you can, as these will only cause you a sense of aggravation at present.

3 FRIDAY
Moon Age Day 14   Moon Sign Aries

Along comes a period during which you can pick up some significant information. It's time to pay great attention, even to apparently casual remarks. You will be amazed at your own resourcefulness and at your ability to make a silk purse out of a sow's ear. Almost everyone is keen to be your friend now.

4 SATURDAY
Moon Age Day 15   Moon Sign Taurus

Although this is the time of the lunar low, such is the power and influence of a number of important planetary positions now, that you will barely notice the slowdown that is usually the inevitable result. Keep plugging away in your efforts to get ahead but accept that your progress is likely to be hindered somewhat and don't allow this to depress you.

5 SUNDAY
Moon Age Day 16   Moon Sign Taurus

It is possible that you find you are running out of steam. Since this is a Sunday, which is usually referred to as being a day of rest, why not take notice of the fact and have a rest? If this proves to be impossible you could at least devote a few hours to social matters and to mixing freely with your friends.

6 MONDAY
Moon Age Day 17   Moon Sign Gemini

Partnerships are likely to take up a great deal of your time as you seem to be in a commanding position with regard to the personality stakes. People gravitate towards you and your popularity is at a peak. Make the most of these trends by socialising freely and by maintaining a high profile at work. Monday morning blues are much less likely for you than they are for your family and friends. Be supportive if others need you to be.

7 TUESDAY
Moon Age Day 18   Moon Sign Gemini

Now you find yourself in a period during which forward planning is not only possible, but also enjoyable too. Although this isn't going to be a crackerjack of a day it does offer some particularly good prospects money-wise. Despite this you should avoid spending too much, except when you come across a bargain.

8 WEDNESDAY
Moon Age Day 19   Moon Sign Cancer

Some matters come to a head now. If you were a salesperson the advice would be 'to close deals carefully'. There is nothing wrong with your mental faculties but you may have to think carefully before taking specific steps. Keep up the social integration and listen to what all sorts of people have to say.

9 THURSDAY
Moon Age Day 20   Moon Sign Cancer

Significant input into areas of life you have stayed away from recently now seems to be the order of the day. You are almost certainly going to be busy today and will have little time to spare for frivolities. When it comes to the boring routines, see if you can find someone to lend a hand and make them more fun.

10 FRIDAY
Moon Age Day 21   Moon Sign Leo

Once more minor opportunities for financial gain pay you a visit. Keep an eye on what you are spending but at the same time understand that you have to speculate a little in order to accumulate later on. Think very carefully before you take any financial risks though. Rewards of a social nature may also come your way, probably because you are so kind at present.

11 SATURDAY
Moon Age Day 22   Moon Sign Leo

The material side of life should be offering everything you need, even if it isn't so easy to get everything you actually want. The weekend is likely to be variable, with perhaps some odd occurrences at times. Further your long-term ambitions by seeking out the right people and chatting to them at some stage today.

12 SUNDAY
Moon Age Day 23   Moon Sign Virgo

The recent planetary thrust has been towards fulfilling your desire for luxury, something that is endemic to the zodiac sign of Scorpio. In your current mood, be careful that you don't end up being accused of hedonism. In the main, you are sociable at the moment and should be mixing freely and happily with all manner of people.

13 MONDAY
Moon Age Day 24   Moon Sign Virgo

A revised plan of action at work could come along today and this could prove to be very timely indeed. Get everything sorted out at work and deal with all those little matters that have been left undone in recent days. By the evening you will be ready to have fun and this should not be hard to find.

14 TUESDAY
Moon Age Day 25   Moon Sign Libra

Finances are likely to be strengthened and you may be able to spend a little more freely than would often be the case. Plans put in place now should work well later, especially with regard to a journey you intend to make months from now. Patience is the key to success and offers great gains – though not for a while yet.

15 WEDNESDAY *Moon Age Day 26 Moon Sign Libra*

You enjoy a very independent approach to life right now. This is fine, just as long as you don't give those around you the impression that you don't want their advice at all. Listen carefully to what you are being told but then go ahead and do what you wish – though as diplomatically as you can manage.

16 THURSDAY *Moon Age Day 27 Moon Sign Libra*

You can open certain doors towards progress at this stage of November. With the Sun still in your first house and everything to play for after a less progressive phase, life should seem fairly fast in pace. Act on impulse, but only when your instincts tell you that this is the right way forward.

17 FRIDAY *Moon Age Day 28 Moon Sign Scorpio*

Decision-making should turn out to be far easier now. The lunar high is very supportive when it comes to mixing with people you know can be good for you. Better luck is on the way and you should be able to indulge yourself in the odd speculation, as long as the risk is calculated.

18 SATURDAY *Moon Age Day 0 Moon Sign Scorpio*

The lunar high continues to support your efforts to get ahead. These may be somewhat curtailed on a Saturday and professional issues especially might have to wait. That doesn't prevent you from having fun, or from making the most favourable impression imaginable on all types of people.

19 SUNDAY *Moon Age Day 1 Moon Sign Sagittarius*

This can be a period of sudden emotional impulses, most of which won't be of any real use to you. Try to stay on an even keel and don't blow up simply because things are not necessarily going your way. Secrets coming your way may be important and you must keep the confidences that others place in you absolutely to yourself.

20 MONDAY
Moon Age Day 2   Moon Sign Sagittarius

Scorpio presently exhibits genuine intelligence and strong acumen when it comes to practical and financial matters. Some may call you ingenious in your handling of business situations. This could lead to a week of potential gains, although it may also leave you short of rest. Balance is everything in life.

21 TUESDAY
Moon Age Day 3   Moon Sign Sagittarius

A few minor disappointments in your love life are possible during this part of the working week. Don't allow these to dominate your thinking. What's needed today is a cool head and strong rational thought. Where you do recognise a few problems, time and your own changing attitude should put matters right.

22 WEDNESDAY
Moon Age Day 4   Moon Sign Capricorn

Energy is not lacking and neither is the ability to size up a situation and act immediately. With reactions like lightning and a strong ability to see 'clear through' the minds of those around you, it might be said that Scorpio is more potent now than has been the case at any time during the year. Make the most of these trends.

23 THURSDAY
Moon Age Day 5   Moon Sign Capricorn

This is a very favourable moment for putting new plans into action. The message is, don't delay. Money matters are simpler to deal with and life carries fewer complications than might have seemed to be the case over the last week or two. Try to avoid unnecessary spats at home, even if you are not the one starting them.

24 FRIDAY
Moon Age Day 6   Moon Sign Aquarius

All of a sudden, your thinking could appear somewhat muddled and your view of the future less focused. Don't panic. As the Moon progresses through your solar third house, you simply need some time off to communicate with those around you and to still your inner mind during what is quite a hectic phase.

25 SATURDAY   *Moon Age Day 7   Moon Sign Aquarius*

If you want to find some relaxation today, look towards home and family. Things are more settled there than they may be in your practical world, which is a potential maelstrom of activity. Give yourself time to reflect on recent happenings and avoid rushing anything if at all possible. Slow and steady is the best way today.

26 SUNDAY   *Moon Age Day 8   Moon Sign Aquarius*

Romantic matters should be amiable and smooth. The closer you get to the end of the month, the more relaxed you are likely to feel, though without losing that vital 'edge'. For perhaps the first time in November thoughts of comfort, relaxation and security could be entering your mind and demanding at least some of your attention.

27 MONDAY   *Moon Age Day 9   Moon Sign Pisces*

You can continue to make the best of prevailing financial strengths and might even gain in monetary terms as a result of something you did a long time ago. Weighing up what makes those around you tick should be quite easy and you can afford to back your hunches in most matters today.

28 TUESDAY   *Moon Age Day 10   Moon Sign Pisces*

Seek out the new and unusual in life if it proves possible to do so at the moment. Anything odd or even downright weird has a specific fascination for Scorpio, and this trait is particularly emphasised at the moment. You might even be able to capitalise on this in hard financial terms if you apply your interest to objects or things which could increase in value.

29 WEDNESDAY   *Moon Age Day 11   Moon Sign Aries*

There are possible gains to be made in a monetary sense, particularly if you keep your eye on the ball and are willing to hunt out that very special bargain. Too much speculation isn't to be advised, but you should recognise a good investment when you see one. It would be hard to fool you in terms of someone's sincerity too.

30 THURSDAY
Moon Age Day 12   Moon Sign Aries

The strongest instinct in your life for today is to make money. Several major planets point in that direction and all of them are saying 'go on, you can do it'. To many Scorpios this will make eminent sense, so if you have been hanging back through lack of confidence, now is the time to apply yourself. Never lose sight of common sense, though.

December

2017

1 FRIDAY
Moon Age Day 13   Moon Sign Taurus

This is a day when you might have to tone down some of your recent efforts. There is no real point in pushing yourself too hard whilst the lunar low is around. To do so leads to frustration and doesn't enhance your chances of success. There are indications that you may learn something surprising about a friend.

2 SATURDAY
Moon Age Day 14   Moon Sign Taurus

Attempts to get on in life could lead to some disappointments because you are still under the influence of that rather negative Moon. Keep your expectations reasonably low and settle for a quiet time. The start of the weekend might not prove to be especially exciting, but it can lead to some unexpected gains.

3 SUNDAY
☿ *Moon Age Day 15   Moon Sign Gemini*

This is a time for capitalising on new opportunities, no matter from which direction you find them coming. Not every line of research that you follow at the moment will lead to a great revelation, though. On the contrary you may find that you will have to dig deep into life at present to get to the truth of matters.

4 MONDAY
☿ *Moon Age Day 16   Moon Sign Gemini*

The practical in life isn't quite so easy to address now as it may have been yesterday. The fact is that you are tied to certain routines that you really can't get away from. Treat these with a little respect but also find moments when you can have some fun. There are financial gains possible as the day wears on.

5 TUESDAY ☿ *Moon Age Day 17   Moon Sign Cancer*

Weigh your options carefully in the balance and don't try to proceed until you know that you are likely to succeed. This is especially important if you are a working Scorpio. Not everyone will appear to be on your side at the moment but the people who really matter should support you fully.

6 WEDNESDAY ☿ *Moon Age Day 18   Moon Sign Cancer*

You will almost certainly be drawn into the new and unusual today. Your thoughts are inspirational and you want to get on and forge new paths. There are some frustrations to be expected along the way but in the main you are frank, free and quite outspoken. Just be careful who you talk to – and the way you approach them.

7 THURSDAY ☿ *Moon Age Day 19   Moon Sign Leo*

You will actively desire to be in the public eye today and can get on very well in almost any sort of company. Practical skills come to the fore and you find yourself able to concentrate much more than has been the case of late. Certain family members bring out your grumpy side now, so stay away from them if you can.

8 FRIDAY ☿ *Moon Age Day 20   Moon Sign Leo*

You might find that outdoor interests are somehow constrained, possibly by practical developments, together with the needs that certain other people have of you. Try to save at least part of the day for doing what suits you and indulge yourself a little if you get the chance. All Scorpios need a dose of luxury now and again.

9 SATURDAY ☿ *Moon Age Day 21   Moon Sign Virgo*

Much is geared today towards practical matters and the way you view them in a moment-by-moment sense. Conforming to expected patterns is rather more difficult than it might have seemed yesterday but you can still force yourself to get on with those who have similar interests and desires. As this is the weekend, these trends are more likely to affect home than work.

10 SUNDAY ☿ *Moon Age Day 22* *Moon Sign Virgo*

Beware of situations that sound too good to be true. In all probability they are. Keep your eyes wide open, particularly if there seems to be too many bargains about and use your common sense at all times. On a less practical note, do some planning now that will make the Christmas period more comfortable for everyone concerned.

11 MONDAY ☿ *Moon Age Day 23* *Moon Sign Virgo*

Your curiosity tends to be powerfully stimulated today and you want to know what makes everything tick. Try to stay away from too much rich food, at least for now, because your digestive system isn't helped by present planetary positions. Family gatherings could be on the cards very soon, so be prepared.

12 TUESDAY ☿ *Moon Age Day 24* *Moon Sign Libra*

This ought to be one of your better days for getting ahead in a general sense and for establishing new patterns of behaviour that are going to be useful for the future. Look at matters carefully but be prepared to act on impulse when you know instinctively that this is the right way for you to proceed.

13 WEDNESDAY ☿ *Moon Age Day 25* *Moon Sign Libra*

Your ego is growing rapidly. Something you have recently done gives you cause to be proud of yourself. Don't let this fact go to your head because pride definitely does go before a fall. There are people around who need your timely advice now. Find out who they are and offer what help you can.

14 THURSDAY ☿ *Moon Age Day 26* *Moon Sign Scorpio*

You are quite assertive at the moment and it would be all too easy to mislead someone as to your true opinions. So often in discussions at the moment, you will take a particular stance, simply for the sake of the argument. In your heart you know that this is never a good idea and it would be far better to tell the truth as you see it from the outset.

151

15 FRIDAY ☿ *Moon Age Day 27   Moon Sign Scorpio*

Most things should fall nicely into place today and over the weekend. The lunar high supports your efforts to get everything done well ahead of Christmas week, and you manage to find time to have some real fun right now. Getting out and about would be good, as would meeting with interesting new people.

16 SATURDAY ☿ *Moon Age Day 28   Moon Sign Scorpio*

In terms of everyday life you find it easy to adapt to the needs and wants of others. The general level of excitement should continue, and with Christmas coming there is little to prevent you from having a very good time. Although this period is not exactly inspirational, it does have plenty going for it with regard to information gathering.

17 SUNDAY ☿ *Moon Age Day 29   Moon Sign Sagittarius*

A period of security and growth begins on this Sunday, although as these trends are new in your chart, you may not recognise it today. The Sun is in your solar second house, the place it always occupies for you at this time of year. Build your dreams slowly because that way they last longer.

18 MONDAY ☿ *Moon Age Day 0   Moon Sign Sagittarius*

A hectic pace is probably not only inevitable but also necessary today. What matters most is communication. You can talk the hind leg off a donkey, but if you can't find one of those, almost anyone will do. Even people you barely pass the time of day with as a rule are now targets for your tongue.

19 TUESDAY ☿ *Moon Age Day 1   Moon Sign Capricorn*

Work and property matter in equal proportion today. With less of a tendency to push the social side of life, it appears that you are finally getting down to doing something concrete. Ignoring all those people who want to drag you off on their own particular form of adventure is not going to be easy, though.

20 WEDNESDAY ☿ *Moon Age Day 2   Moon Sign Capricorn*

All sorts of communications typify today. You could be on the telephone a lot, or else busy on the computer or mobile. The chances are that you are using every possible means to keep in touch with others, even with loved ones who are far away. Conforming to physical expectations could be somewhat tricky today as you are in more of a thoughtful mood.

21 THURSDAY ☿ *Moon Age Day 3   Moon Sign Capricorn*

Every Scorpio needs luxury sometimes and today is as good a time as any to get it. Although you might find it difficult to leave others to enjoy the cut and thrust of social situations, you would take well to a break from activity. The best of all worlds would be a sauna or a health spa of some sort in order fully enjoy today.

22 FRIDAY ☿ *Moon Age Day 4   Moon Sign Aquarius*

This is a time for social highlights, through business as well as family and friends. Maybe it's an office party, or some sort of gathering after work. Whatever it turns out to be you will be happy to be the life and soul of the party. Beware, though, that the same trends from earlier in the month continue, so too much eating or drinking might be a mistake.

23 SATURDAY *Moon Age Day 5   Moon Sign Aquarius*

There are entertaining experiences coming your way this weekend. It's true that you love to be in the limelight at the moment, so there is a strong possibility that half the fun in your vicinity is being created by you personally. If you are well ahead with your work, take some time out to do what pleases you.

24 SUNDAY *Moon Age Day 6   Moon Sign Pisces*

There are various ups and downs to deal with at home, though in the main you manage to maintain your sense of humour and even get up to some mischief yourself. There could be some good family news coming your way, even though you may find it to be surprising. Scorpio is very creative on this Christmas Eve.

25 MONDAY

Moon Age Day 7   Moon Sign Pisces

It is entirely likely that Christmas Day will find you in generally good spirits and able to cope with the domestic demands of the day. Most of you will be on your best behaviour and will show the naturally affectionate side of your zodiac sign. Some of the presents you receive could be howlers, but don't let that offbeat sense of humour show.

26 TUESDAY

Moon Age Day 8   Moon Sign Pisces

Boxing Day is likely to be hectic but very enjoyable. It seems you want to talk to just about anyone who comes your way and you remain cheerful and optimistic in your general state of mind. Your confidence certainly isn't lacking and you can look out for a few really unexpected surprises.

27 WEDNESDAY

Moon Age Day 9   Moon Sign Aries

You may be prone to especially high ideals or even certain illusions regarding your own life. Talk to people who are in the know and be prepared to learn from what they have to say. If you are feeling somewhat under the weather today you are likely to find that a breath of fresh air would do you good.

28 THURSDAY

Moon Age Day 10   Moon Sign Aries

The fun principle is strong for your zodiac sign as the holidays progress. Not everyone treats you as their cup of tea but that's part of the problem of being a Scorpio – most people adore you but a few people definitely don't. There isn't much point in trying too hard when the latter situation is the case.

29 FRIDAY

Moon Age Day 11   Moon Sign Taurus

On a practical level you are nowhere near as capable as you seemed to be yesterday. Don't worry because the things you can't or won't do will be dealt with by someone else. If you really feel that you have contributed everything you can to the holidays, sit back and enjoy watching everyone else work for a change.

30 SATURDAY   *Moon Age Day 12   Moon Sign Taurus*

You are filled with bright ideas at present. What is likely to be lacking is the necessary energy to put many of them into practice. Although you will want to make the running socially, even here you could easily run out of steam. By tomorrow, you should be getting back to normal and in the meantime you can watch life go by.

31 SUNDAY   *Moon Age Day 13   Moon Sign Gemini*

In a social sense it is possible that you will feel somewhat disheartened at the start of today. Scorpio people are not universally ones for New Year parties but you can get yourself into the right state of mind if you put some effort into doing so. For the sake of others, and ultimately for your own enjoyment, try to have a good time.

RISING SIGNS FOR SCORPIO

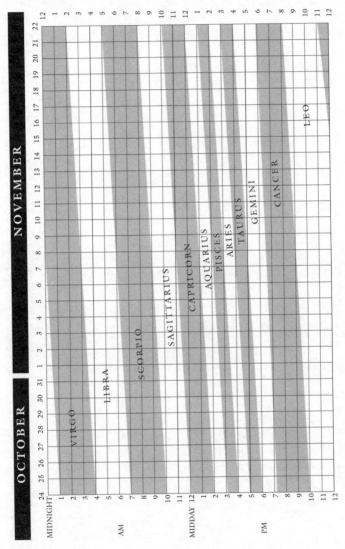

THE ZODIAC, PLANETS AND CORRESPONDENCES

The Earth revolves around the Sun once every calendar year, so when viewed from Earth the Sun appears in a different part of the sky as the year progresses. In astrology, these parts of the sky are divided into the signs of the zodiac and this means that the signs are organised in a circle. The circle begins with Aries and ends with Pisces.

Taking the zodiac sign as a starting point, astrologers then work with all the positions of planets, stars and many other factors to calculate horoscopes and birth charts and tell us what the stars have in store for us.

The table below shows the planets and Elements for each of the signs of the zodiac. Each sign belongs to one of the four Elements: Fire, Air, Earth or Water. Fire signs are creative and enthusiastic; Air signs are mentally active and thoughtful; Earth signs are constructive and practical; Water signs are emotional and have strong feelings.

It also shows the metals and gemstones associated with, or corresponding with, each sign. The correspondence is made when a metal or stone possesses properties that are held in common with a particular sign of the zodiac.

Finally, the table shows the opposite of each star sign – this is the opposite sign in the astrological circle.

Placed	Sign	Symbol	Element	Planet	Metal	Stone	Opposite
1	Aries	Ram	Fire	Mars	Iron	Bloodstone	Libra
2	Taurus	Bull	Earth	Venus	Copper	Sapphire	Scorpio
3	Gemini	Twins	Air	Mercury	Mercury	Tiger's Eye	Sagittarius
4	Cancer	Crab	Water	Moon	Silver	Pearl	Capricorn
5	Leo	Lion	Fire	Sun	Gold	Ruby	Aquarius
6	Virgo	Maiden	Earth	Mercury	Mercury	Sardonyx	Pisces
7	Libra	Scales	Air	Venus	Copper	Sapphire	Aries
8	Scorpio	Scorpion	Water	Pluto	Plutonium	Jasper	Taurus
9	Sagittarius	Archer	Fire	Jupiter	Tin	Topaz	Gemini
10	Capricorn	Goat	Earth	Saturn	Lead	Black Onyx	Cancer
11	Aquarius	Waterbearer	Air	Uranus	Uranium	Amethyst	Leo
12	Pisces	Fishes	Water	Neptune	Tin	Moonstone	Virgo